THE PROP EFFECTS GUIDEBOOK

In *The Prop Building Guidebook*, author Eric Hart demonstrated how to cut, glue, sculpt, and bend raw materials to build props. Now in *The Prop Effects Guidebook*, he shows us how to connect and assemble components and parts to make those props light up, explode, make noise, and bleed. It delves into the world of electricity, pneumatics, liquids, and mechanical effects to teach you how to make your props perform magic in front of a live audience. The book is complemented by a companion website featuring videos of how to create individual prop special effects: www.propeffectsguidebook.com.

Eric Hart is the props master for Triad Stage in North Carolina. He is the author *of The Prop Building Guidebook: For Theatre, Film, and TV*, also published by Routledge. Eric has built props for numerous theatres on and off Broadway and throughout the United States. He has worked with some of America's top actors, directors, and designers at the Santa Fe Opera, the Actors Theatre of Louisville, and the Public Theater. Eric has also constructed props for display and exhibition including the holiday window displays at several major New York City retail stores.

D1612132

THE PROP EFFECTS GUIDEBOOK

LIGHTS, MOTION, SOUND, AND MAGIC

ERIC HART

Routledge
Taylor & Francis Group

NEW YORK AND LONDON

First published 2018
by Routledge
711 Third Avenue, New York, NY 10017

and by Routledge
2 Park Square, Milton Park, Abingdon, Oxon, OX14 4RN

Routledge is an imprint of the Taylor & Francis Group, an informa business

© 2018 Taylor & Francis Group

The right of Eric Hart to be identified as author of this work has been asserted by him in accordance with sections 77 and 78 of the Copyright, Designs and Patents Act 1988.

All rights reserved. No part of this book may be reprinted or reproduced or utilised in any form or by any electronic, mechanical, or other means, now known or hereafter invented, including photocopying and recording, or in any information storage or retrieval system, without permission in writing from the publishers.

Trademark notice: Product or corporate names may be trademarks or registered trademarks, and are used only for identification and explanation without intent to infringe.

Library of Congress Cataloging-in-Publication Data
A catalog record for this book has been requested

ISBN: 978-1-138-64113-6 (hbk)
ISBN: 978-0-203-72939-7 (ebk)

Typeset in Univers
by Keystroke, Neville Lodge, Tettenhall, Wolverhampton

Printed in the UK by Severn, Gloucester on responsibly sourced paper

Visit the companion website: www.propeffectsguidebook.com

contents

preface

Every props person is called upon to perform magic at some point in their career. Your props may need to move, shine, bleed, burn, sing, and break.

Some shows are notorious for the effects required: the actor who is shot with a crossbow in *Deathtrap*; the floating vase in *Blithe Spirit*; the pan filled with firecrackers in *You Can't Take it With You*. Other stage effects appear in a multitude of shows: a sink with running water; a crying baby; a cup that breaks.

Researching prop effects can be difficult. A book on robotics quickly delves into electrical components and programming that is far more complex than theatre will ever need. A website on sound often deals with speakers much larger than can fit in your props. Prop effects require a breadth of knowledge across many disciplines, but rarely need the depth. You do not need to engineer a bridge or design a computer: you just need to know how to make a few tricks work in a way that will fool your audience, keep your actors safe, and make your production manager happy.

The Prop Effects Guidebook is one of the first attempts at providing a comprehensive look at all types of prop effects. Other prop books may have a chapter or two on tricks; you can also find books on theatre effects that deal with large-scale solutions for the scenery and lighting departments. Finally, the world of props gets its own book that reveals the magic we do. The titles of the chapters give you an indication of what kinds of effects we will cover.

I intend this book to work hand-in-hand with my other book, *The Prop Building Guidebook: For Theatre, Film, and TV*. This book does not dwell on how to build the prop itself, nor how to cut and shape any raw materials, such as wood or metal, to make these effects work. All of that is covered in much more detail in *The Prop Building Guidebook*, allowing this book to cut straight to the chase with the effects themselves. This book is all about making your props *do* something.

acknowledgments

This book would not be possible without the continuing support of my wife and occasional collaborator, Natalie Taylor Hart. She maintained endless patience as I performed all manner of science experiments in the dining room.

Like most props people, my knowledge has come from everyone I have worked with; I am just one more stop in the endless march of props expertise that has been passed on from generation to generation since the beginning of theatre. I do want to thank a few people who have helped me with specific technical knowledge while writing this book: Seán McArdle, Zach Murphy, Taylor Dankovich, and Sean Dane. I also want to acknowledge the combined knowledge of the members of the Society of Properties Artisan Managers (S*P*A*M), whose expertise I have referenced many times throughout this book and who have helped me answer numerous questions, whether they knew it or not. Likewise, I would like to thank the members of the ControlBooth internet forum and the Tech Theater subreddit.

Special thanks go to all those who contributed photographs to this book: Kylie Clark, Patrick Drone, Jay Duckworth, Elizabeth Friedrich, Rick Gilles, Kari Hagness, Lori Harrison, Erin Kehr, Darin Kuehler, Helena Mestenhauser, Andreea Mincic, Eimer Murphy, Todd Peacock-Preston, Alec Thorne, Nancy Wagner, and Pam Weiner.

Finally, I want to thank the team at Taylor and Francis who helped make this book possible, especially my editor, Meredith Darnell, and Stacey Walker, who has been with me every step of the way since I proposed my very first book way back at USITT in 2011.

one

designing, prototyping, testing

Some trick props are straightforward and can be solved by duplicating an existing solution: adding an electric candle to a lantern, running water to a sink, or making a breakaway glass. Other trick props can be more complex, either because the effect needed is out-of-the-ordinary, or because the context of your production prohibits more traditional solutions. This book provides the building blocks for potential solutions, but you will need to design, prototype, and test the actual prop by yourself.

When approaching a trick prop, many prop builders follow a process similar to the following:

1.   Define the Problem
2.   Specify Requirements
3.   Research and Brainstorm Solutions
4.   Develop a Solution
5.   Build a Prototype
6.   Test and Redesign

You do not always need to follow these steps in order or do each one. You can design something, test it, and find a problem, then return to an earlier step for modifications. Let's look at each step in turn.

Figure 1-1: This magical music box needed to light up on the inside and have a puff of smoke emerge on cue. The crank on the front needed to be turned by the actor as well as move on its own. The whole thing had to be cued from the light board as dancers carried it all around stage. That is a lot of magic for the box, but once the problem is fully defined, it can start to be broken down into individual challenges.

Define the Problem

The first step with any prop effect is to define the problem. Gather as much information as possible from the beginning. The script has clues as to what the prop needs to do. The director and designers will have ideas about the trick prop as well. Always talk to them first as they may deviate from the written stage directions.

They may be vague ("the piano should be a bit magical") or they can be specific ("we want the front leg of the stool to break when he sits on it"). When discussing the trick, use this time to further define what exactly is needed ("does he need to be able to sit on the stool before the moment it breaks?"). If you have an idea that requires them to stick to a certain plan, bring it up now ("if the exploding clock is hung on the upstage wall, we can have a crew member trigger it manually from behind").

Specify Requirements

Once you have exhaustively described what your trick prop needs to do, you should have a list of requirements you need to meet. If a solution does not meet all of those requirements, then you need to improve the solution or come up with a different one.

In the world of live performance, a prop effect will have additional considerations which may or may not have been discussed in your meetings with the director and designers:

1. Reliability
2. Reset Time
3. Cost
4. Triggering
5. Back-up Plan
6. Sightlines

Reliability – You want your effect to work each and every time it is used, and you want it to act the same way whenever used. Sure, in live theatre, something will go wrong every once in a while: cues are called late, actors misplace a prop, and raccoons run across stage. If your effect fails because of a freak accident, that's fine, but if it fails because it was built poorly or inadequately tested, that's on you.

Make your prop intuitive in its operation so others can figure it out when you are not around. The crew should be able to tell when the prop is set and when it has successfully operated. This way, if it fails, it will be easier to figure out why. Give visual and tactile clues to guide its operation. For example, if you need to turn a crank to operate it, make the crank unable to turn past its "on" and "off" position. If the prop uses electricity,

put an LED indicator light so you know whether the prop is getting power or not. For a spring-loaded prop, there should be a satisfying "click" to know that it is loaded and ready to go.

Think about the ease of use and the amount of operator training it takes to use your prop successfully. If it is operated by a crew member who calls in sick right before a performance, will the replacement crew member be able to learn it in a short period of time? Again, make the operation as intuitive as possible. If you need to push a series of buttons and switches in a specific order, arrange them from left to right in that order.

Finally, make the prop easy to repair. If the prop has batteries, they need to be accessible to change them. Incandescent light bulbs also need to be reached. Do not lock these parts inside solid structures; sometimes, adding a small access panel or door is necessary. If you have other parts that may wear down or break, such as strings, rubber bands, or belts, build your prop so they are removable, rather than gluing them to some inaccessible surface.

Reset Time – If you want to have flower petals gently fall from the sky throughout the final scene of your play, you will have to clean them all up before the next show and load them back into the petal-dropping device. How long will this take to do? This will become the crew's responsibility, and it will take them away from their other duties, or it could potentially lead to higher labor costs if the effect requires them to come in early every day.

If your theatre has more than one performance per day, such as a matinee and evening show, the effect needs to be able to be reset in between shows, which can be as short a time as an hour or two. Again, the running crew need to be able to do their other duties and often need a meal break in between shows as well.

Designing effects which are easy to reset can be even more challenging than designing the effect itself. For some effects, you may need multiple props that can get you through several performances; the crew can reset all of them at once during a less-busy time.

Cost – Every prop needs to fit within your budget. For your trick props, consider the cost of experimenting and prototyping as well as the cost of building the actual prop. Second, determine the cost per use. A prop which uses consumables, such as confetti, fog fluid, and batteries, will cost money every performance. Even a few cents' worth of materials can add up over a multi-week run. Finally, consider the cost of repairs. For some props, you may wish to build a backup or two so the crew can swap them out when irreparable damage occurs. This is not always possible. If the cost of a potential repair exceeds your budget, you may wish to consider a different solution, or at least provide a back-up plan that the production and design team is okay with.

Triggering – A prop effect can be triggered by a crew member, the stage manager, an actor, or automatically. Each of these has its advantages and disadvantages, and what you choose depends on your specific set of circumstances.

Having a crew member trigger the effect will only work if a crew member is available. Check with stage management. The effect may be happening during a busy sequence where all the crew members are busy with something else, or they may need to be in other locations where they cannot get to the prop in time.

A stage manager may trigger an effect if it is possible to run a button to the booth. The disadvantage is that they are not on stage and may not have the best vantage point to make sure the prop is properly set or that it can be triggered without harming anyone nearby.

On the surface, having an actor trigger their own prop seems like the best solution because they can perfectly time it with their own action. However, the triggering action needs to be effortlessly smooth, intuitive, and reliable. Some actors have trouble operating a standard door knob while on stage. You want the actor to be focused on bringing their character to life and telling a story to the audience, not on jiggling a finicky switch to make a crossbow fire. A second problem with actor-triggered props is that if something goes wrong, it can break their focus, or worse, cause them to start improvising as they attempt to fix the problem.

Automatic triggering of a trick prop may occasionally be useful in theatre, but it is rare. We usually want a human in charge to get the timing just right. Automatic triggers also run the risk of going off at the wrong moment before everyone on and backstage is ready.

Back-up Plan – The cast, crew, and stage management need to know what to do if the effect does not work. If a decorative lighting or smoke effect fails to trigger, the show may continue uninterrupted. If a prop fails to make a sound effect, the sound operator should be ready to play a back-up sound cue through the regular speakers.

Other tricks can potentially prevent the performance from continuing. A magic door which fails to open will leave the actors stranded on stage: it should have a second way of opening without "magic" involved. A pair of trick handcuffs should not actually immobilize an actor's arms: they should be built with an unlocking mechanism which the actor themselves can trigger.

The failure of a trick prop absolutely cannot put anyone in danger of harm. At worst, a prop failure should be a bit of an awkward moment where the audience realizes something went wrong and the actors improvise through. We have all heard the story (or one similar) where an actor's fake gun fails to go off, so he proceeds to club the other actor to death with it. The show goes on.

Sightlines – A trick which is triggered by pulling ropes will not work if that prop is out in the middle of the stage with nowhere to hide the ropes. Electrical props need to be battery-powered if you do not have anywhere to hide power cords. In a proscenium space, you can hide a crew member behind a wall to trigger a prop; you cannot do this in-the-round. Always consider what the audience can or cannot see when designing your effect.

Besides the needs of the director/designer/playwright and the special considerations for trick props, your prop has all the needs of a regular prop as well. Remember to fulfill your prop's aesthetics and physical characteristics. Aesthetics include the design style, period, color, transparency, sheen, and overall size. Physical characteristics include its strength, weight, impact resistance, water resistance, and inflammability.

Research and Brainstorm Solutions

At this point, you have a big list of problems your prop needs to solve, and you have probably already begun thinking of ways to achieve that. Now is the time to really dive in and come up with potential solutions.

Come up with as many possible solutions as you can. The more the merrier. Do not be afraid if they are way out in left field. Even rejected ideas may come in handy for prop problems in the future. Do not settle on your first idea. It may work, but you may have missed a simpler or more elegant solution.

Ideas come from research and brainstorming. Let's look at research first.

Other props people are the most invaluable research source you can have. If you have a network of others in the field, you can keep track of who is good at electronics, or who recently put a sink on stage. They can point out potential pitfalls, suggest parts and materials, or refer you to another props person with more knowledge.

The employees at supply and hobby shops can also be helpful for research. If you need to make a remote control vacuum cleaner, talking to the people at a remote control car shop can help you narrow down the types of components. Some vendors may even get so excited at your project that they experiment with some of their parts to see if they can solve the problem for you.

The internet is full of websites and communities that can help. Chances are, if you need to make a trick prop, someone has already made something similar and put the instructions online. Instructables.com is a great central repository of projects, while YouTube.com has many "how-to" videos of props and tricks. The Cosplay community shares many tips on integrating LEDs and microcontrollers into projects, and the Halloween and Haunted House industries are a good source for information on pneumatics and animatronics. Other helpful communities center around model trains, and RC planes, cars, and boats.

Successful brainstorming involves asking questions. How do existing products solve your problem? As you take apart and analyze existing products, you build a mental library of mechanisms, techniques, and clever tricks. Can you combine parts to make a new solution?

Use analogies between your prop and random objects. You may notice solutions that would not have come to mind when you compare your problem to an entirely different situation. Ask yourself, "How is my prop like this random object?" or "How would I solve my problem using this random object?" The movement of an oscillating fan might be used for a sweeping surveillance camera. Props people can often be found holding up a hose from the plumbing aisle to a plastic waste bin from the cleaning aisle, ignoring the bewildered stares of the store's employees.

When brainstorming, it can be helpful to ask others in your shop for ideas, or even to get a small group together for a brainstorming session. This can even involve other departments if your prop needs to light up or make sound, for instance.

Develop a Solution

Once you have a solution for your trick prop, you are ready to start developing it. To review, make sure your solution answers these questions satisfactorily:

- Have you met the director/designer/playwright's requirements?
- Is your solution safe to build, use, store, and dispose of?
- Can you obtain all the materials and equipment you need within your budget and deadline?
- Do you have enough time to complete your prop before technical rehearsals?

Remember you need extra time for troubleshooting and fixing problems.

A good solution is elegant. It will have the fewest parts possible, since more parts mean more opportunities to fail. It will be as simple as possible, and not rely on parts that need to be more precise than you can make, or a trigger that is too finicky for an actor to use consistently. A good solution is robust, working smoothly in conditions far tougher than what it will be subjected to on stage. It will be aesthetically pleasing. You will have the skills to be able to complete it.

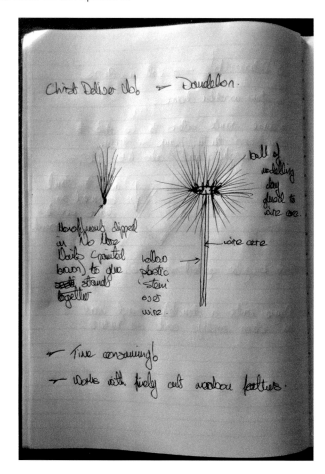

Figure 1-2: This drawing was created as the prop builder's design for a fake dandelion flower which the actor could blow the seeds off. *Christ Deliver Us!* Abbey Theatre, 2010. Photo courtesy of Eimer Murphy.

During this phase, you will make drawings, models, and prototypes to refine and improve your solution. Often, you may not have the best idea of how your parts will work together. Some aspects will be more uncertain than others. Start with the most uncertain parts. For instance, if you need to make a cuckoo clock that breaks apart and makes a noise, you may find that the breaking apart is the tricky part, while the noise is easily accomplished with a wireless speaker. Figure out the breaking first before spending time on the sound. You may discover that the breaking mechanism only leaves room for a specific size of speaker.

Drawings help you remember what ideas you have. They can help you think through all the steps and make notes of what order you need to go in or what uncertainties you need to solve. For some props, you may even want to work on a CAD drawing to figure out the precise shape and size of the pieces and see how they all fit together.

Models can be helpful to work through a solution on a larger prop without having to build a full-scale prototype. It can help you find proportions and see how things work together in three dimensions. A scale model will not be a perfect replica though; materials have more bend and give as they are scaled up.

Scale models will also let you practice techniques and pick up on any unforeseen variables before committing to the full-scale version.

Build a Prototype

A prototype is used as a reference to build the final prop. You can quickly test your solution with materials that are easy to work with but less durable than your final materials. You can also iron out all the bugs before

Figure 1-3: A prop prototype built out of Meccano-Erector pieces. *Crazy For You*, Elon University, 2012.

you spend time sculpting and painting the exterior of the prop. A prototype is also helpful when you need multiple copies of a prop, so you can make up a parts list or even instructions for others to duplicate your work.

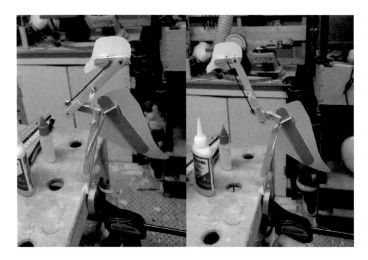

Figures 1-4 and 1-5: The initial movement and mechanisms for these bobbing pigeons were worked out with popsicle sticks, paper, and rubber bands. Once perfected, the parts were measured, drafted, and produced on a 3D printer, while the bodies were sculpted and vacuum formed. *The Producers*, Omaha Community Playhouse, 2016. Photos courtesy of Darin Kuehler.

Sometimes, the prototype itself may be integrated into the final prop if it solves all your problems.

For mechanical and moving props, working with basic materials speeds up the process. Materials which are cut with basic hand tools, such as cardboard, foam core, wire, popsicle sticks, and straws can help you quickly determine sizing, spacing, shapes, and proportions for all sorts of mechanisms. You can also use hobby construction sets, such as LEGO, K'Nex, Meccano-Erector, and Tinker Toys.

Electrical circuits may be prototyped using breadboards (covered in the next chapter). Alligator clips and other temporary connectors can also help get your circuit working correctly before you spend a lot of time cutting wire to size and soldering components together.

If you need to work with pneumatic cylinders, motors, or other electro-mechanical components, assemble them temporarily with Velcro, hose clamps, cable (zip) ties, or hanging strap (plumber's tape).

Test and Redesign

Play with your prop a number of times to make sure it is consistent and reliable and does what it needs to. Don't play nice: remember that your actor will be running on adrenaline in front of a full audience, with bright stage lights beaming into their eyes. Have others test your prop if necessary; it can be very illuminating to watch others interact with a prop, to see if they fumble when trying to flip a switch or discover some imaginative way to make it fail. A trick prop should be usable by everyone, not just yourself.

For a trick prop that requires actor involvement, get a working prototype into rehearsal as soon as possible. Sometimes this involves a special rehearsal session where you teach the actor(s) how to use the prop. It is helpful to watch them use it or to receive detailed notes on its usage so you can pinpoint potential problem areas and improve them while there is still time to rehearse. With proper planning, the actors can be comfortable using a fully-functioning trick prop before they even get into technical rehearsals.

When you provide something in rehearsal, you get feedback on an actual object; you can demonstrate real materials doing real things, and tell the director, "This is what this does. What are your thoughts?" The prototype can spark further questions and suggestions, and you can realistically discuss the potential compromises or problems that may crop up. Sometimes you get lucky,

and the director or actor realizes that a slight change in blocking can solve some of your problems and make the ultimate solution easier on your end.

Sometimes, several prototypes can be beneficial. When the director or design team do not have a clear image of the reality of a prop, build two to four samples and present them. It is easier for most people to compare existing items and offer specific suggestions on them than it is to describe a purely imaginary item.

Samples and prototypes do not always need to be shared in person. Images and video can be recorded in your shop and sent to directors or designers before the rehearsal process even begins. This is especially useful for theatres that work with out-of-town creative teams.

Figure 1-6: Introduce prototypes for actor-manipulated trick props as soon as possible into rehearsal.

Sometimes, you need to scrap a whole prototype and start over; if you begin early enough, you have time to work on something else.

Not all trick props require you to work through each step of this process. Sometimes you know exactly how to solve the problem from experience; other times the solution is just obvious. It does not hurt to think through each effect, even if you just imagine a prototype in your head rather than building a whole sample prop. The remaining chapters deal with the methods you will use to create these effects. You do not need to read them in order, but they do build on each other; for instance, you need to know about electricity to deal with lighting, and you need to know about both pneumatics and electricity to deal with some liquid delivery effects.

two

electricity, wiring, soldering

Electricity is the foundation of many prop effects. You need to understand electricity, not just for lighting and motion, but for pneumatic elements, sound equipment, and remote controllers as well. All of these are covered later in their specific chapters; this chapter covers the basics of electricity, how to hook up different components, how to make and troubleshoot circuits, and how to do it all safely.

What is Electricity?

The fundamental nature of electricity is complex: we use metaphors to help describe it. Many of these metaphors are not entirely correct at all times. However, 99 percent of the electrical props we build can be figured out with a very basic knowledge of electricity.

Imagine that an electrical circuit is a bicycle chain. The pedals are the power source, like a battery or a plug in the wall. When you turn the pedals, the chain moves and spins the wheel. If the chain is broken, the wheel will not spin no matter how fast you pedal. This is one of the fundamental rules of building electrical props: you need a complete path, or **circuit**, from the positive (or live) end of a power source to the component (such as a light or a motor) and back to the negative (or neutral) end of the power source. The "chain" cannot be broken.

Now imagine that the bicycle is upside-down and the wheel is free to spin. If you place your hand lightly against the bicycle tire as it spins, you will slow it down and your hand will start to heat up. The person pushing the pedals is still pushing as hard, but the wheel is not going as fast. Your hand provides resistance to the wheel. All components, such as lights or motors, provide **resistance** to the circuit. Instead of changing the energy into heat, they turn it into light and movement.

The voltage moves electrons through the wires and components. This movement or flow is called **current**. Electrons only flow when their path, or circuit, is unbroken from the positive side of the battery to the negative side.

Volts, Amps, Watts

We need to know how electricity is measured, so we know how to get the proper amount of power to a component, how to make sure a battery will not die in the middle of a show, how to avoid damaging our parts or catching them on fire, and how to keep safe.

The **force** of electricity is measured in **volts** (V). **Watts** (W) are how much power is released each second. **Amperes** (A), or "amps" for short, are the amount of electricity flowing through the wire. These three measurements relate to each other in an equation commonly called "West Virginia":

$$W = V * A$$

The force is provided by either a battery or **mains electricity** (the electricity running through your house and theatre). AA and AAA batteries provide 1.5V of force. A car battery provides 12V. The voltage of mains electricity differs by country; the US and Canada use 120V, while the UK and Australia use 230V. The electrical components and devices you use will only operate within a small range of voltages. You cannot power an LED straight from the mains, nor can you run a ceiling fan straight from a car battery. We will talk about how to alter the electricity to make that possible a bit later in the chapter.

Your components and devices should specify how much wattage they consume. For example, a 100-watt light bulb uses 100 watts. Your mains electricity should have circuit breakers to limit the amount of amps it provides. If you try to power too many devices on a single circuit, you can draw so many amps that the wire can melt or a fire can start. A circuit breaker turns off the circuit before that happens. Most of the wall outlets in your home lead to a 5-amp circuit, while some can be a 10- or even 20-amp.

Using the "West Virginia" equation, we can see how many 100W light bulbs we can plug into a 20-amp circuit without tripping the breaker, assuming the voltage for our mains is 120V.

$$W = 120V * 20A$$
$$W = 2400W$$

Therefore, 2,400 watts is equal to 24 100W light bulbs. If your components draw more watts than your power source or your wires are meant to handle, then something is going to heat up and fail, or even catch fire.

Ohm's Law

Resistance is a measure of how difficult it is for the electrical current to push through a material. All materials have resistance, from lights and motors, to switches and wires. In our bicycle wheel example, placing your hand on the wheel adds resistance. You can either pedal at the same rate and allow the wheel to spin more slowly, or pedal harder to keep the wheel spinning at the same speed. Ohm's Law is an equation that shows the relationship between resistance, current, and voltage:

$$V = I * R$$

Voltage (V) equals current (I) times resistance (R). Current is in amperes, and resistance is in ohms (Ω). This is useful for determining what type of resistor to use to convert voltage to what a component needs. Props people use this a lot for LEDs, so we will work on some examples in the next chapter.

AC/DC

Electricity flows in one of two ways: direct current (DC) and alternating current (AC). In general, AC power comes from the plugs in the wall, while DC power comes from batteries.

In our bicycle metaphor, DC power spins the chain in a circle. AC power rapidly wiggles the chain back and forth.

Most components are designed to work only on AC or on DC. An AC motor that is given DC power won't run, and may even be damaged or cause a fire. LED tape meant for DC power will flicker and burn out within hours (or even minutes) when powered with AC. Some equipment may operate for a short period of time, but will still eventually fail.

When ordering parts, the catalog should specify whether the part runs on DC or AC when listing what voltage it operates at. While 12VDC is 12 volts DC, 120VAC is 120 volts AC.

Figure 2-1: A wall wart is an AC to DC transformer attached directly to a plug. The label should say what kind of power it outputs. This one provides 12V and 2A. You can attach any kind of connectors you want to the end, or solder the wires directly to your prop.

You can turn AC power into DC using a **transformer**; if the electric cord for your device has a "wall wart," it is transforming the AC power to DC. This is useful when you build a prop with DC components but it does not need to be portable. If your prop is plugged in, you do not have to worry about batteries going dead. A wall wart also allows you to plug into a dimmer that is controlled by the theatre's light board.

DC power is converted to AC power using an **inverter**; a cigarette-lighter adapter with an Edison outlet on the end is an example of a common inverter. EL wire, for instance, can only operate with AC power. You may also need one if you need to run small kitchen gadgets, like a toaster, off a battery.

A variable benchtop supply can be useful when prototyping. This allows you to select between a range of different voltage (typically between 0V and 30V). Once you figure out how much power your prop requires to operate successfully, then you can choose the batteries or AC adaptor that fits the bill.

Electrical Safety

The amount of electricity required to harm you depends on a multitude of factors. With the power sources we use for props, though, DC above 30V is potentially harmful and above 48V is considered lethal, while AC power should be considered deadly.

Non-lethal electricity can still shock or surprise you. It may startle you and make you hit something above or behind you. Electricity can heat metal enough to burn you. People with heart conditions and other medical issues are more vulnerable to harm from electricity.

- Always work with the power source disconnected
- Check that no bare wires or connectors are in contact with metal
- Do not touch bare wires unless you can personally verify they are disconnected from power
- Avoid wet conditions
- Do not wear metal jewelry

Voltage alone is not an indicator of danger. A Van de Graaff generator does not kill you even though it is producing over 100,000 volts. However, the current it produces is below 100μA (microamperes). It is the combination of voltage and current that harms the body. Touching a 9V battery to your tongue sends about 1.3 mA (milliamperes) through your body, which is over ten times as much current.

- Use tools with insulated handles
- Only touch potential live circuits with one hand to avoid having the electricity run from one hand to the other, through your heart.
- Disconnect a plug by pulling on the connector, not the cable.

When you build a trick from scratch, you can be sure all the parts are in good working order and all the wires are sound. When you are repurposing parts, you are less certain that everything is fit and safe. Antiques can have wiring that is not as safe as modern insulated wiring, or components that are more dangerous.

Batteries

Batteries are a simple source of portable power but come in a wide variety of shapes, sizes, and styles. Choosing the right battery can be the difference between success and failure in your prop project. The following chart shows the properties of different types of batteries we use.

Carbon-zinc, alkaline, NiCd and NiMH batteries come in various sizes labeled AAA, AA, C, and D. Each of these are a single cell, providing 1.5V of power. Larger sizes last longer. Higher voltage batteries are made up of multiple cells connected together; for instance, a 9V battery is made of six to eight small cells, depending on the type. A 6V flashlight battery has four individual cells inside.

Sealed lead-acid batteries are commonly used in cars, motorcycles, RVs, and boats. They usually provide 12V and will last a very long time for props, though they are very heavy. Motorcycle batteries are much smaller than car batteries.

Lithium ion batteries are found in laptops, cell phones, and cameras, and can be small enough for hearing aids. They come in a wide variety of voltages

Battery	Nominal volts per cell	application	recharge	internal resistance	notes
Carbon-zinc	1.5	low demand, flashlights	no	moderate	cheap, old technology
Alkaline	1.5	small motors, circuits	no	high	most commonly available
Rechargeable alkaline	1.5		yes	high	alternative to regular alkaline
High-capacity alkaline	1.5	can handle larger current demands	no	low	more expensive
Nickel-cadmium (NiCd)	1.2	medium and high current demand	yes	low	being phased out due to toxicity
Nickel metal hydride (NiMH)	1.2	high current demand	yes	starts low, increases as it is recharged many times	high capacity, pricey
Lithium-ion (Li-ion)	3.6 (common but not standard)	high current demand	yes	high	expensive but very lightweight
Sealed lead-acid (SLA)	2.0	very high current demand	yes	low	heavy, but high capacity

and capacities. Though the most expensive, they are the lightest for the power they provide. The variety of shapes and sizes they come in make them easy to fit in the strangest of places.

Some types of batteries are rechargeable. Always use the correct battery charger. Otherwise, you may damage the charger, the battery, or even start a fire. A great source for props are rechargeable battery packs for RC applications. They are usually high capacity and come in a variety of voltage outputs useful for the kinds of projects we are building.

Battery capacity is measured in **amp-hours**; a single amp-hour delivers one ampere for one hour. A battery with a rating of five amp-hours (5Ah) can provide up to 5A continuously for one hour, or 1A for five hours (or 2A for 2½ hours, and so on). Small batteries use milliamp-hours (mAh or mA).

Alkaline and lithium-ion batteries have a high **internal resistance**, so they cannot dump all their current in a short period. Lead-acid, NiCd, and NiMH batteries have a low internal resistance, so they can empty their full charge in a few minutes. Some components require extra current when first turned on. Motors are notorious for this: a 1-amp motor may actually require several amps for 100–200 milliseconds when first turned on. In this case, a battery with a low internal resistance is needed.

The actual voltage of a battery can vary as much as 10 to 30 percent of what it is rated for. A 1.5V cell may deliver 1.65V when it is fully charged and 1.2V toward the end of its life. Different batteries lose voltage at different rates. NiCd, NiMH, and Li-ion stay fairly flat before suddenly discharging completely. Alkaline has a slight curve down. Lead-acid has a long gentle curve down.

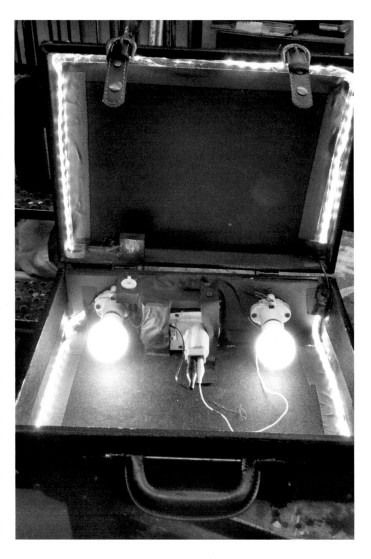

Figure 2-2: The battery for a cordless drill is another good power source. They have a high capacity, are rechargeable, can withstand large draws, and you already have them in your shop. Here, an 18V battery powers LED tape and two light bulbs. A refrigerator door switch turns the circuit off when the suitcase is closed. Photo courtesy of Helena Mestenhauser.

Circuits

A circuit is an unbroken path. It starts at the positive side of a battery or the live wire of mains electricity, travels through all your components, and returns to the negative side of the battery or the neutral wire of the mains. You can have diverging branches or use switches to choose between multiple paths, but each line needs to return back to the power source.

With a **polarized** component, the electricity must flow from positive to negative, so you need to hook up the positive side to the positive wire and the negative side to the negative wire. Examples of polarized components include LEDs and motors (some motors only work when hooked up the right way; others will spin in different directions depending how they are hooked up). With a **non-polarized** component, it does not matter which way it gets hooked up. Examples include wire, incandescent bulbs, and switches.

With AC power, attach your switches to the live, or "hot," side. This way, you do not have power running to components when the switch is off. If you were to touch an element while grounding yourself out, you could be electrocuted. For instance, if you touch the metal part of an empty light socket while holding onto a metal railing, you will get a shock.

With DC power, it matters less where you put the switch: if you ground yourself out touching a live wire, you probably will not injure yourself. However, it is good practice to keep your switches on the positive side. It will develop the habit so you automatically do it when you are working with AC.

Anything that offers resistance to the free flow of electrons in a circuit is called a **load**. Loads include lamps, motors, speakers, and anything else you want to power.

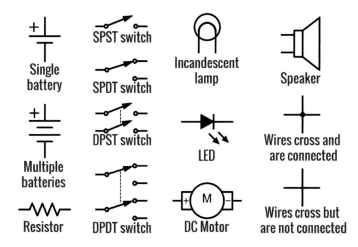

Figure 2-3: Just a few examples of symbols used in circuit schematics. You may find slight variations in the symbols.

Circuit Schematics

When working with electronics, you will find people draw schematics of their circuits using a variety of symbols. While you do not need to learn how to draw circuit schematics to make your own circuits, it can be helpful to know when reading someone else's schematic of a circuit you wish to duplicate or modify.

Parallel vs Series

When you are connecting multiple components, you can either connect them in a line, one after the other, or have multiple wires branch out from one point to all your components. Each of these methods yields different results, and understanding the difference is one of the foundations of building electronic props.

Why does each light receive half the voltage? Why doesn't the first light get all the voltage and

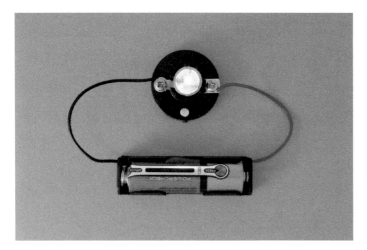

Figure 2-4: A single AA battery provides 1.5V. When we hook up a 1.5V lamp to it, it shines happily at full brightness.

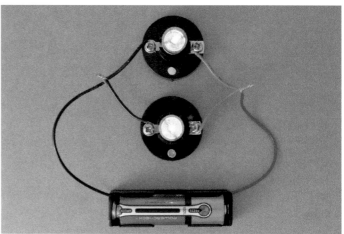

Figure 2-6: If we branch out the circuit and make two separate paths, the sockets are now connected in parallel. Each lamp receives 1.5V and shines at full brightness. Because we have two lamps, the battery drains twice as quickly as when one lamp is connected.

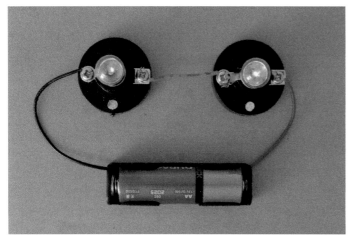

Figure 2-5: When two sockets are connected one after the other, we say they are connected in series. The voltage provided by the battery is split equally between both sockets, so each lamp only receives half, which in this case is 0.75V. This makes the lights shine at half brightness.

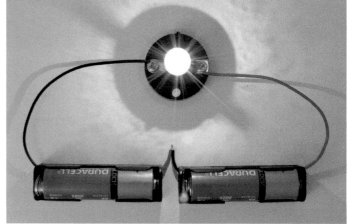

Figure 2-7: The most common way to connect batteries is in series. This increases the voltage. We have two 1.5V batteries, so our lamp is receiving 3V of power, which makes it shine twice as brightly and risks burning it out. Battery holders connect the batteries in series; a four-battery holder will give you 6V, an eight-battery holder will give you 12V, etc.

eidcity, wiring, soldering

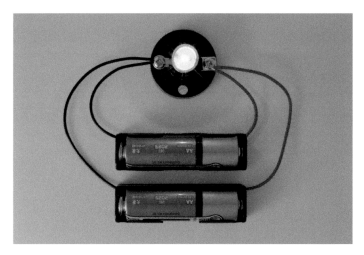

Figure 2-8: Connecting the batteries in parallel will provide the proper 1.5V to our lamp, and it will last twice as long. If one of the batteries dies, the other will continue providing power. This is a useful trick if a prop needs to remain on for a long period of time.

the second get none? Think back to our bicycle metaphor at the beginning of the chapter. If we hold our hand against the wheel, the entire chain slows down. Holding our hand against the wheel is akin to applying a load to the circuit. We can have a bunch of wheels run off the same chain. If you slow down the chain, all the wheels will slow down. This is how a series circuit works: the voltage is split evenly between all loads in the series.

Series connections are how old strands of Christmas lights were wired. If one lamp is removed or burns out, all the lamps connected in series will turn off. If you take out either bulb in Figure 2-5, the other will go out as well.

Another feature of parallel connections is that if one of the bulbs in Figure 2-6 burned out or was removed, the other would continue to stay lit.

Batteries can also be connected in series or in parallel.

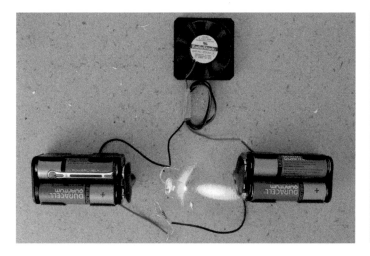

Figure 2-9: More complicated circuits will have multiple parallel connections, with components connected in series within each one. In the above circuit, the LED needs 6V to operate, while the fan needs 12V.

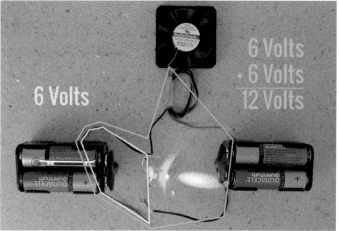

Figure 2-10: This circuit has two parallel paths, each with a series of components. The yellow path connects one battery pack to the LED, giving it 6V. The green path connects two battery packs to the fan, giving it 12V.

Wires

Wires allow electricity to flow from one place to another. Most wire you find is copper; other materials can be used, but will have different properties from what we discuss here. Wire is typically insulated with plastic. Allowing the bare wire to touch other bare wires or to touch metal parts of your prop can keep it from operating correctly or cause a short circuit which can heat up and catch fire or damage the electrical components in your prop.

Wire can be either stranded or solid. **Stranded** wire is a bunch of thinner wires bundled together. It is more flexible and can withstand movement and repeated bending. **Solid** wire is a single piece of metal. It is more compact and cheaper, but only comes in shorter lengths. It is most commonly used in circuit boards, where space is at a premium, and where no movement of the wire should occur.

In North America, wire size is specified by AWG (American Wire Gauge). Smaller numbers indicate thicker wires. Since stranded wire has gaps, the actual overall diameter will be slightly larger than solid wire of the same AWG. Most wire strippers will indicate both solid and stranded gauge sizes for each hole. In North America, 24AWG can be one strand of 24 AWG wire (1/24) or seven strands of 32 AWG wire (7/32); the full appropriate specification for stranded wire will be 24 AWG 7/32.

In Europe, wire size is given in cross-sectional area in square millimeters (mm²). It can also be given by the number of strands of wires of a diameter in millimeters. For instance, a 7/0.2 wire has seven strands of wire which are each 0.2mm in diameter. This example has a cross-sectional area of 0.22mm².

Proper electrical wire should have the size printed or embossed along the insulation. If not, you have to strip the insulation, count the number of strands, and measure their thickness with a micrometer or vernier calliper. There are charts to help you convert from diameter to gauge, or for finding the gauge of stranded wire (for example, seven strands of 26 AWG will always be 18 AWG).

The wire needs to be thick enough to handle the amps you are running through it. Wire will heat up if it carries more current than it is made for.

The following chart shows the more common wire gauges you will use in props:

Application	AWG#	metric (mm²)
prototyping and breadboards	22	0.35
lamp cord	18	1.00
common residential light fixtures	14	2.00
common residential small appliances	12	3.00

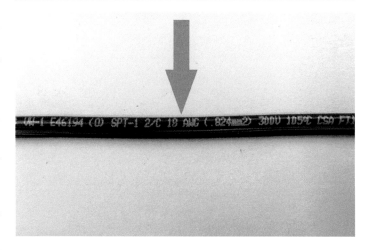

Figure 2-11: It is not always easy to see, but proper wire should have the gauge printed or embossed on the insulation. Here, you can see this is 18 AWG wire. To the right is the equivalent metric size: 0.824 mm².

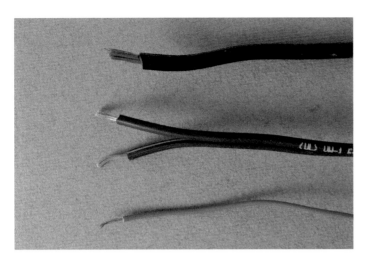

Figure 2-12: From top to bottom: 14 AWG wire, 18/2 AWG wire, and 22 AWG wire.

Any copper wire with insulation can be used for wiring, such as speaker wire and phone cords. As long as you know the gauge, you can figure out how much current you can pass through it. The main difference with proper electrical wire is that the insulation is rated for the high temperatures which electricity can generate. Speaker wire and phone cords can melt from too much voltage. Use them for low-voltage (under 30V) projects only.

Magnet wire is coated with a very thin layer of insulation. This needs to be scraped or sanded off to reveal the wire; chemicals can also remove the insulation, depending on what the coating is. Magnet wire holds its shape when bent and is useful in very tight spaces.

Zip-cord is two (or more) cables held together by insulating jacket that can be separated by simply pulling apart. Lamp cord usually comes in zip-cord form; 18-gauge zip-cord would actually be referred to as 18/2, since it has two 18-gauge wires. Some zip-cord uses two different colors for the insulation, making it useful to keep track of which wire is the positive and which is the negative.

The insulation color of your wires does not affect the wires themselves. Certain colors have become standard for various purposes. In DC circuits, red and white are positive, and black is negative. Other colors can be used to differentiate additional positive connections.

The colors of wires in AC circuits depend on which part of the world you are in.

Stripping a wire means removing the outer layer of plastic and exposing the bare wire. Good wire stripping will leave just enough wire exposed to securely connect it to the component or connector, without nicking or gouging the actual wire itself.

Using a knife or scissors risks damaging the metal wire underneath the insulation. And using your teeth to strip the wire may be a handy trick to know when you need to repair a prop five minutes before the curtain goes up, but should not be used when you have the time and resources to do it properly.

	US	Europe
safety ground – earth wire	green, green and yellow stripes, or bare copper	green and yellow stripes, or bare copper
Neutral	white or gray	blue
Live	black	brown
second hot wire	red or blue	

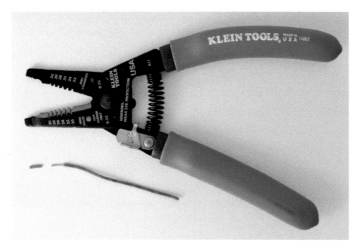

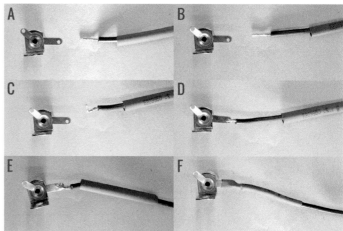

Figure 2-13: A good quality wire stripper is needed, particularly for smaller gauge wires. General hardware-store strippers may not go small enough, or may not work as well as higher quality electrician snippers.

Figure 2-14: A) Strip the end of the wire and slip a piece of heat-shrink tube over it. B) Tin the wire by heating the exposed copper for a second, then touching the soldering wire to it. C) Bend it, then D) insert it through the hole of the lug and crimp it tight, making a good mechanical connection. E) Solder it on both sides. F) Cover with the heat-shrink tube.

Soldering

Soldering joins wires together with melted metal. It provides a stronger connection than wire nuts or crimped connectors. The melted solder flows between all the strands of the wires, making a solid connection, which allows for more efficient transmission of electricity and keeps moisture out.

Solder is reversible, but not readily so. Do not solder together a connection that needs to be plugged and unplugged regularly.

Soldering takes practice to perfect. The most important tip is to heat the metal, not the solder. Melted solder will flow into hot metal, but will just bead up on cold surfaces.

For small components and thin wires, you will use a soldering iron. You can find hundreds of different shapes and sizes of tips to go on a soldering iron. Many of them have interchangeable tips. Tips for different brands of irons may not be compatible with each other so pay attention to what you buy. The three most useful types for props are:

- Chisel tip – The broad tip evenly delivers heat to component leads and pads. Solders wires, through-hole components, and surface-mount components. Used for desoldering too.
- Conical tip – Good for precise work, like very small surface-mount components.
- Bevel or hoof tip – Can hold a lot of melted solder, which is useful for soldering multiple pins on a surface-mount chip at once, or connecting small-gauge wires together.

Figure 2-15: A third hand will hold the two pieces you want to solder together so your hands are free for the soldering iron and solder. Many come with a magnifying glass to help you work on small components.

For larger wiring projects, a **soldering torch** can speed things up.

Insulating Your Wire

As you build an electrical prop, you will end up with areas of bare wire that need to be covered.

As the name implies, **heat-shrink tube** is a tube that shrinks when heated, either by a heat gun or a light touch with a soldering iron. If the right size is used, it will cling tight to whatever is inside it, and conforms to irregular surfaces. It provides electrical insulation, protects the wire from dust and moisture, and gives mechanical strain relief.

Besides being used on connections and splices, it can also be used over a wire that has its insulated sleeve worn off or damaged. It comes in different colors so it can help color-code the circuit. It can even be used to bundle multiple wires into a single cable.

Electrical tape can be used to insulate bare metal as well. It does not provide the strain relief that heat shrink does, and the adhesive may fail over time. If not done right, it does not really give a seal against environmental factors either. Electrical tape is quick and does not require additional tools, while heat shrink is superior for more permanent situations.

Some props people use a dab of **hot glue** to insulate bare connectors. This is usually fine for low-voltage DC circuits; avoid it on anything run from the mains. You should still solder or mechanically reinforce the connection, as too much jiggling can eventually break the hot glue free. Avoid it on components that heat up, like incandescent light bulbs or transistors, as they will remelt the hot glue.

Connectors

An electrical connector allows you to join wires and components together mechanically, without soldering. You may have times when you need to remove part of your circuit for maintenance or replacement during the run of your show, or you may want to build a circuit that can be taken apart after the show and the parts reused without having to desolder a bunch of joints.

Crimped connectors use a crimping tool to join the connector to the end of the wire. The metal in the connector is folded around the wire, leaving no gaps or spaces. A good crimp will not let air in, which would bring moisture and cause corrosion.

Crimping requires a proper crimping tool, not a hammer, pliers, vise, or other makeshift tool.

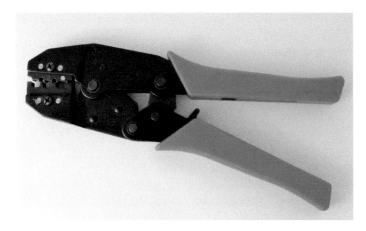

Figure 2-16: As you squeeze the handles of a ratcheting crimper together, the jaws stay closed. When enough pressure has been applied, the jaws will open and release the crimped part.

Crimping is mostly done with stranded wire. Solid wire is hard to conform to the shape of the terminal and can become weakened through crimping.

For pre-insulated terminals, the color standards are:

* Red Insulation 0.5-1.5mm^2 / 22-16 AWG
* Blue Insulation 1.5-2.5mm^2 / 16-14 AWG
* Yellow Insulation 4.0-6.0mm^2 / 12-10 AWG

It's almost impossible to "over-crimp" a connector. If the connector pulls apart from the wire, the crimp was not done properly. Always test it before assembling your circuit. Better to fail now than during a show.

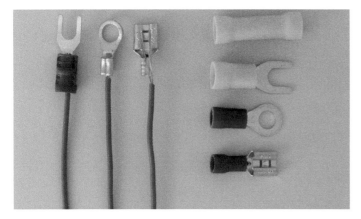

Figure 2-17: Crimp connectors come in a variety of styles and sizes. A properly crimped connector should look like the wire on the left. The one in the middle shows what it should look like underneath the insulation. The wire fits snugly in the barrel; the end of the wire barely sticks out above the crimp; and the wire insulation is stripped to just before the crimp. The wire on the right highlights some mistakes: the end of the wire extends too far past the crimp, the insulation is removed too far away from the crimp, and not all the strands of the wire are inside of the crimp.

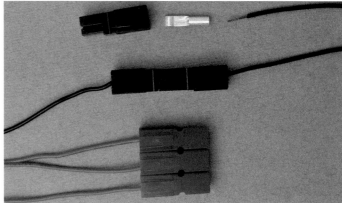

Figure 2-18: A Powerpole connector is genderless, and does not have male or female ends. Each connector can mate with any other connector. The wire is crimped into a spring clip, which is pushed into the back of the plastic housing until it locks in place. The housings have dovetail slots on the sides which allow you to join multiple connectors together.

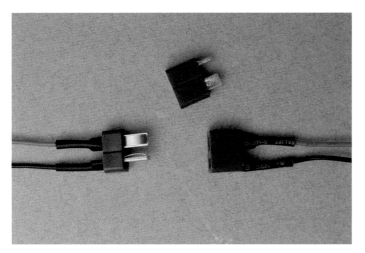

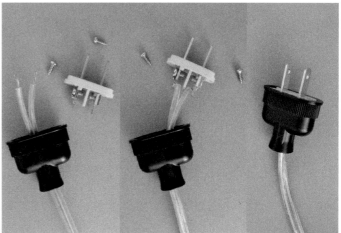

Figure 2-19: A Deans connector is a popular type of T plug used with RC battery packs. The wires are soldered to the tabs in the back which are then covered with heat-shrink tube. The configuration of the T plug prevents you from connecting the two halves in the wrong direction.

Figure 2-20: You can find a variety of ready-to-use plugs that attach to lamp cord. The plug above separates into two parts. Feed the lamp cord through the housing first. Attach the ends of the wires to the screw terminals on the ends of the blades. Pull the connector back into the housing and screw it together.

Adding a Plug

With an AC powered prop, you need a plug to connect it to a wall outlet. The type of plug you use will differ according to what country you are in.

With Edison plugs and many other types of mating connectors, the **male** end has the exposed metal pins while the **female** end is the recessed receptacle. Standard practice is to put the female end on the power source and the male end on the device being powered. When adding your own connectors, you should stick with this practice to avoid confusion and electrocution. A powered male plug will shock anything it touches with its bare metal end. Remember: the female brings the power.

Switches

A switch mechanically connects and disconnects wires. The **actuator** is the exposed part of the switch that you use to flick it on and off. Many types of actuators exist. Common ones include toggle, push button, slide, rocker, and lever. A knife-switch is like a Frankenstein switch, with all exposed metal.

The number of terminals on a switch has to do with the number of poles and throws it controls. The **pole** is the number of circuits the switch controls, and the **throw** is how many positions each of the switch's poles can be connected to.

An SPST is the simplest switch. It hooks up between the positive side of the battery and the load. It turns the load on or off.

Figure 2-21: Examples of a push button switch (A), roller switch (B), slide switch (C), and toggle switch (D). These switches have different numbers of terminals to hook wires to. "A" has two terminals, "B" has three terminals, and "D" has six terminals.

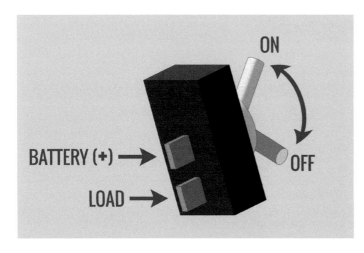

Figure 2-22: SPST – Single Pole, Single Throw. Two terminals.

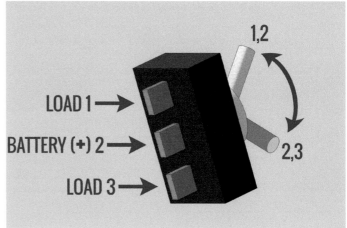

Figure 2-23: SPDT– Single Pole, Double Throw. Three terminals.

An SPDT switch selects between two loads. The battery hooks to the center terminal. One load attaches to each remaining terminal. The switch controls which of the two loads gets power.

Most SPDT switches are known as "ON-ON," which means the actuator has two positions and one of the circuits is always connected. Another type is "ON-OFF-ON," which means the actuator can stop in the middle and turn both circuits off.

A DPDT switch is essentially two SPDT switches operated simultaneously. Three terminals act as one SPDT switch, and the other three act as a second switch. The two sides can even be different voltages because they are independent of each other. You can use it as a SPDT switch by ignoring one row of terminals in a pinch.

Since reversing polarity is a common use for DPDT switches, you can find special DPDT crossover switches, which only have four terminals, two for the battery, two for the load (two for the input, two for the output). The criss-cross wiring is internal to the switch.

A **DPST** switch also has four terminals. Switches with larger numbers of poles and throws usually use numbers in their abbreviation, like 3PDT, 4P3T, 5P4T, etc. The larger numbers of throws are more likely to be rotary switches.

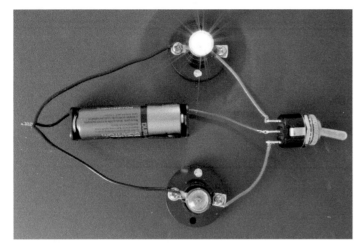 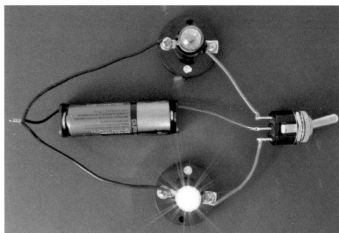

Figures 2-24 and 2-25: An SPDT switch in action.

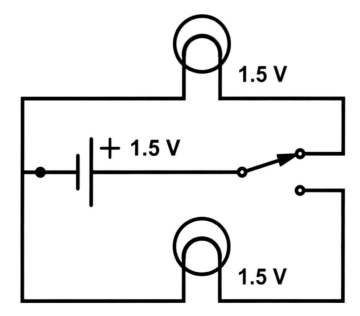

1.5 V

+ 1.5 V

1.5 V

Figure 2-26: The circuit schematic for the SPDT switch in Figures 2-24 and 2-25.

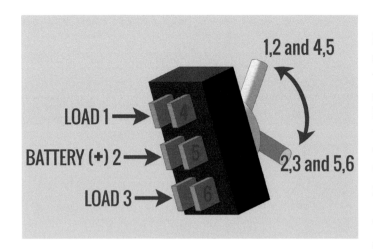

Figure 2-27: DPDT – Double Pole, Double Throw. Six terminals.

A switch is either maintained or momentary. A **maintained** switch remains in its state (either on or off) until you change it. Toggle and slide switches are certainly maintained; some push buttons stay on when you push them, and only turn off when you push them a second time.

A **momentary** switch only remains actuated as you press it. Normally-open (NO, or push-to-make) means the circuit stays open (power does not flow) until you press the switch. This is the most common type of momentary switch used in props. Normally-closed (NC, or push-to-break) means it is on until you push it. Refrigerator lights operate on NC momentary switches.

Many other kinds of switches exist for more esoteric prop needs. A pull chain switch is used in many types of lighting fixtures. Another handy one is the **reed switch**, which activates in the presence of a magnet. These can be useful when you need a switch without seeing an actor hit a button, like setting a lantern on a table or when a tracked prop reaches a certain point.

You want the switch to be easy to locate in the heat of the moment but not in a position where it will accidentally be triggered. You usually want some nice tactile feedback so the actor using the prop can be certain they switched it. Some switches have built-in lights to indicate when they are "on," which can be good for providing certainty backstage as to whether they are working, but not good for onstage if the light can be seen (particularly if it is supposed to be a vintage prop from a period before light-up switches were invented).

A **relay** is a switch which is controlled electrically. You can use low-voltage power to turn on a high-voltage component, or vice versa. Props people use them either to have a battery-powered microcontroller activate a mains-powered prop, or to have the light board activate a DC prop that is plugged in. We will talk about them in greater detail in Chapter 11: Control.

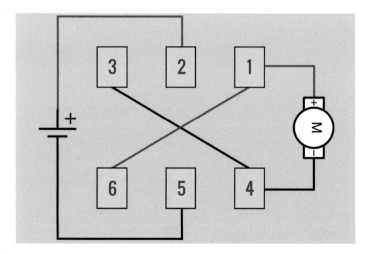

Figure 2-28: Another use for a DPDT switch is to reverse the polarity of a component, like a DC motor that can spin in either direction. Connect the wires according to the diagram to make a switch that changes which way the motor spins.

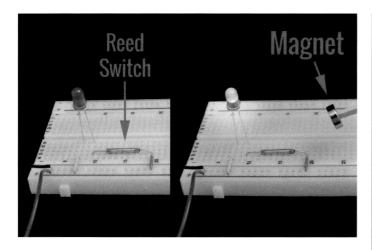

Figure 2-29: A reed switch activates in the presence of a magnet. This is a normally-open reed switch, which turns on when a magnet is near. You can also buy a normally-closed reed switch, which is on all the time but turns off when a magnet is near.

Breadboards

A **breadboard** is used to prototype and test a circuit. The most commonly used type is a solderless breadboard, or plugboard, which is a plastic block with many perforations where wires can be repeatedly inserted and removed. Because it is reusable and does not involve soldering, it allows you to quickly assemble components into a circuit to see if an idea will work. If the prop is not subject to rough handling, the circuit can even remain on the breadboard during the run, and be disassembled at the end so the parts can be reused.

The perforations contain spring clips to keep the wires secure when inserted. Use 22 AWG solid wire to connect parts to the breadboard. Some components have pins which match the standard spacing of a breadboard's perforations and can be attached directly.

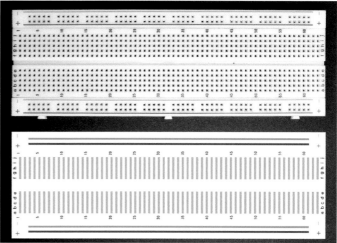

Figure 2-30: Various breadboards share many similar features, though smaller ones may have less than what is pictured. The diagram below the photo shows how the various perforations are connected. The blue and red rows along the top and bottom are called bus strips and are meant to provide power to the components. Connect the positive end of a battery to one of the perforations in the red row and the negative end to one in the blue row and you can draw power from any of the other perforations in the row. The green columns are terminal strips, and the five perforations on either side of the gap are connected to each other. If you place a wire in column 1, row f, it will be connected to something plugged in column 1, row h, but not to something in column 1, row b. The gap through the center is to accommodate certain components that have pins on either side.

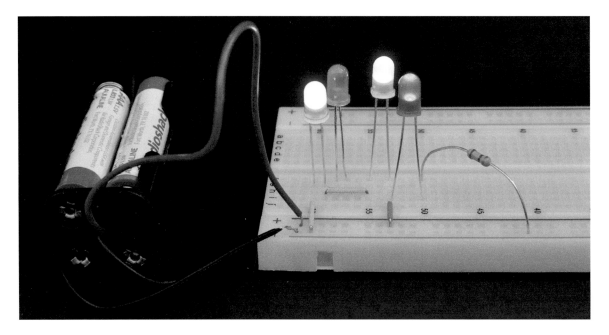

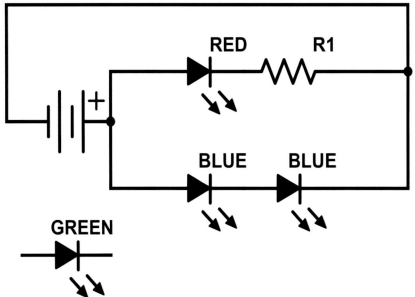

Figures 2-31 and 2-32: The breadboard in this photograph is the same as this circuit schematic. We have two parallel circuits; one has a red LED and a resistor in series, while the other has two blue LEDs in series. The green LED is not actually connected to anything, so remains dark.

Components

We have already introduced some components that are commonly used by props people such as switches. Lights and resistors will be discussed in great detail in the next chapter.

As your prop-building prowess advances, you may want to introduce **sensors** to add some interactivity and responsiveness to your props. Sensors can be triggered by light, movement, pressure, magnets, sound, and many more exotic things.

A **capacitor** is charged with electricity much like a battery, except it can release it all at once. This is useful for props that need a short burst of higher-voltage energy. Props people commonly use capacitors when building camera flashes, which will be discussed in the next chapter.

When purchasing components, you often have several choices as to their physical form. One important property is the **terminal style**, or how you connect it to everything else. A quick glance at a catalog will show dozens or even hundreds of terminal styles, most of which are described with acronyms. Luckily, we only really need to know a few.

The smallest of components will be either surface-mount (SMD) or through-hole (PTH).

Surface mount is made to solder directly to a printed circuit board (PCB). These components sit flat and are usually very small and delicate. PCBs are a bit over-advanced for props purposes; however, it is possible to solder wire to SMB components to use them without PCBs.

Through-hole is for going through a hole in a PCB and soldering to a pad on the other side. It can also be used on a **breadboard**. Many of the LEDs and resistors you find come with through-hole terminals. These are much easier to solder a small wire to.

Slightly larger components may have solder lugs or screw terminals. Some may have wires leading out of them. These are the easiest to hook up, though if you snip all the wires off, you lose the ability to connect them to anything.

Solder lugs are more heavy-duty pieces of metal made to solder single or stranded wire to. A pierced solder terminal has a hole in it for the wire to pass through. If the wire is too big for the hole, it means you are using too large a wire for that component.

In a **screw terminal**, the wire is held by tightening a screw. Strip enough insulation off the end of the wire so only bare wire is under the screw. If you are using stranded wire, twist the strands so they stay together. Bend the end of the wire into a half-circle, like a candy cane. Hook this directly under the head of the screw so the open area faces the right and tighten the screw. Some styles of screw terminal crimp the wire between two plates, so you do not need to do all of this.

A **panel mount** component is meant to be attached to an enclosure or thin panel so the main part is on the outside while all the wiring is on the inside. They usually have a round body with a nut so you can drill a hole in your panel or enclosure, feed the component through, and then tighten the nut on the other side to hold it secure. Panel mount switches are especially useful when adding lights to metal lanterns.

Voltage Drop

The longer the wire, the more resistance it has. An incandescent bulb at the end of a 100-foot wire will be noticeably dimmer than the same bulb at the end of a 1-foot wire.

For most props, the voltage drop is negligible. Most components can operate within a small range of voltages, and your wires need to be dozens of feet long before you have to realistically worry about voltage drop.

Connectors also add resistance, and loose or corroded connectors can add even more. Remember that batteries lose voltage as they are depleted, so older batteries can also cause a voltage drop.

To reduce voltage drop:

- Shorten the wire
- Use thicker wire for long runs
- Use the least number of connectors possible.

three

lights

Props versus Electrics

Most theatres have a master electrician who handles all the stage lights. If a prop needs to light up, is that the responsibility of the props department or the electrics department? The answer varies wildly from theatre to theatre, and even from show to show. In general, a props department is responsible for all the parts that are "seen," and the electrics department is responsible for running all the cable backstage to hook it up to the light board. If a practical table lamp has a plug that is seen by the audience, the props department may add it on, but if the cable runs offstage, the electrics department will add one of their stage pin plugs. In some theatres, the props department may need to do everything to make a prop "plug and play." In others, they may need to do nothing.

So while this chapter will explain everything about making a prop light up, the props department at your specific theatre may not be responsible for all of it.

Bulbs and Bases

The variety of light bulbs out there are nearly endless. They operate at different voltages and wattages. They come in many different sizes and shapes with different base styles. The size of the housing or fixture can limit the size and/or shape of the bulb you choose.

Other variables include their color temperature (if white) or color and whether they are clear or frosted. They have a beam angle which ranges between a tight spotlight and a more general wash. You can even find different filament designs if you need a vintage look (thankfully there are LEDs that are now mimicking the appearance of vintage incandescent light bulbs).

Technically, a light bulb is called a **lamp**. Not all lamps are bulb-shaped, so "bulb" is not always an accurate description. Your electricians may give you flack if you say "bulb." However, props people need to deal with table lamps and floor lamps. Technically, these should be called light fixtures, light fittings, or **luminaires**. That term is a bit broad, though, and props people deal with specifics.

I find that when a props person says "lamp," they are referring to either a table or floor lamp. So, in this book, I use the term "light bulbs" to avoid confusion with the common household lighting fixture. The electricians among you may protest, but it helps prevent ambiguity in this chapter.

Finally, you can choose between incandescent, halogen, LED, fluorescent, and CFL (compact fluorescent) bulbs. In rarer cases, you may need a metal halide or sodium vapor bulb for your prop.

Props rarely use the LED bulbs used in homes; they are not historically accurate for most time periods, their quality of light is different from incandescents, and they do not dim smoothly. In props, we use individual LEDs, LED tape, and other products, all covered later in this chapter. CFLs are also rare to find on stage. The bulk of your bulbs for practical light fixtures like table lamps will be incandescent and halogen, both of which give off lots of light and are easily dimmed.

With props, you sometimes need to be concerned about the visual appearance of the bulb itself, not just the quality and quantity of its light. You may find yourself using an incandescent bulb even if LEDs would be cheaper and brighter.

Be sure to have backups of your bulb in case it breaks or burns out, or at least use a bulb that can be bought locally or shipped quickly. You don't want to build your prop around a vintage bulb which has been discontinued, especially after the director and designers have fallen in love with it.

In many cases, the lighting designer chooses the bulb and the master electrician purchases it. Still, you should be aware of what types of bulbs are out there for use in your props. Electricians know about bulbs for their stage light fixtures, but may be unaware of the myriad specialty and miniature bulbs that a prop may use, or where to buy them. A props person may want to have a few specialty bulbs on hand to give a show-and-tell to the electrician or lighting designer when deciding what to use.

The shape and size of a bulb is indicated by a letter and a number. The number will give the diameter in eighths of an inch, so "8" is equal to 1 inch in diameter, and "16" is equal to 2 inches in diameter.

Common bulb shapes include:

- **A** (Arbitrary) – an inverted pear shape, very common in North America. A19 is the iconic household bulb. A smaller size is A15, used in appliances.
- **C** (Candle) – looks like a candle flame. C7 and C9 are common Christmas light bulbs.
- **G** (Globe) – a perfect sphere. G25 is used around the archetypal dressing-room mirror.
- **MR** (Multifaceted Reflector) – a format for halogen bulbs, such as the very popular theatrical bulb, the MR16.

- **PAR** (Parabolic Aluminized Reflector) – another popular theatrical bulb used for creating soft pools of light.
- **T** (Tubular) – these can be fluorescent tubes (T8 and T12) or used to describe LEDs (a 5mm LED is also known as a T1-3/4).

Some bulbs are also specified by a three-letter ANSI code, which indicates its properties. For instance, an EXT lamp is a 50-watt MR16 with a 15° beam angle. An EGE is a 500-watt T-4 lamp. The code is arbitrary; you don't really need to know what is what, other than that an EXT lamp will be the same kind regardless of who manufactures it.

Figure 3-1: Lamp sockets come in a wide variety of sizes, forms, and mounting options. They are also built to handle different power levels and temperatures, so be sure to use one that will not melt or catch fire with your bulb.

The bulb will also have a base indicated by another code. Again, the letter refers to the type, while the number refers to the size. Some types of bulbs are only found with specific bases, while others can come in a few different bases.

- Edison (E) – Screw-in base. E12 is known as the candelabra base, used for chandeliers and decorative lighting. E17 is an intermediate base, historically used for Christmas bulbs. E26 is the standard household bulb size (it is E27 in Europe, though most bulbs can fit either base).
- Bayonet (BA) – These are pushed into the base, then twisted to lock into place.
- Bi-pin (G) – Two pins that are pushed into place. They can have a second letter in the code to further define them; for instance the most common base for an MR16 is a GU5.3 base.

Color Temperature

With light sources, white is never really white: some whites are "warm," or appear to have a yellow or amber tint, while other lights are "cool," and have a slightly blue tint. **Color temperature** is a comparative measurement using degrees Kelvin to indicate how warm or cool a light source is: 2,000K to 3,000K is warm white, 3,100K to 4,500K is cool white or bright white, and above 4,500K is daylight.

Our eyes adjust to the ambient light on stage; whatever is the most neutral appears to be **relative white**. Differences in color temperature are most noticeable when we have a small light source that deviates from this relative white. For instance, if the stage is lit with

Examples of color temperature for common light sources

1,850K	Candles
2,400K	Standard incandescent
2,800K	Halogen
3,000K	Photo studio lights
4,000K	"Natural" white
5,000K	Camera flash, fluorescents
6,000K	Sunlight

soft candle light, a lamp with a halogen bulb will appear noticeably cooler, and may even seem blue

When choosing lights, be sure to pay attention to the color temperature your lighting designer wants. Bulbs and LED strips will indicate what their color temperature is, and you need to know whether you are trying to match existing lights or deviate from them.

Theatrical Lights

I will not get into the variety of theatrical lighting fixtures you will find at your theatre: you can find far more comprehensive books on the subject, and it is unlikely you will need to deal with them. However, a few miniature fixtures sometimes find their way into props.

A **PAR Can** is the housing for a PAR lamp. A **birdie** is a nickname for the smallest type of PAR Can, a Par 16. They typically take either PAR16 or MR16 bulbs. Two of the most common voltages are 12V and 120V.

An **inky** or **inkie** is a nickname for a 3″ Fresnel instrument. They typically use an ESR lamp (100W, 120V halogen with a bayonet base).

Figure 3-2: A birdie shown next to a standard light bulb for scale.

Running a Lamp on a Battery

If you are building a circuit with DC components, then making a lamp run on a battery is quite simple.

If you need to run a regular household lamp off a battery, it gets a bit trickier. This happens when the lamp is on a moving piece of scenery that cannot have a cord, or when the crew does not have time to plug it in during a quick scene change.

> An inverter can be used to run an AC-powered lamp from a battery, but an inverter loses some power in the process. Most inverters are only 50 to 95 percent efficient, and some will drain the battery even when the light is off.

You cannot power a regular household light bulb off a battery; it was made for 120V. If you try, it will heat up but it will not glow. You have several options powering a lamp with a standard base (E26) with a battery:

- 12V bulbs for RVs and boats can fit regular sockets. Incandescent versions are not terribly bright and generate a lot of heat. LED ones give out more light, but many do not have the visual appearance the designer may want.
- Adapters allow you to fit a 12V halogen in an E26 base. Halogens are usually the brightest option for low-voltage dimmable lamps.
- You can change the whole base socket. Of course, the next time you use that lamp, you may want it to run on AC again.
- If the lamp has a shade or the bulb is otherwise hidden, you can run a separate cord and base along the side. This is especially useful if the lamp is old and you do not trust the internal wiring.

 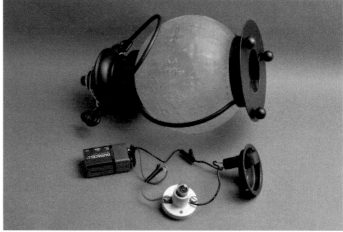

Figures 3-3 and 3-4: Let's review. Find an area on the lantern for a switch that is easy for the actor to find but difficult for the audience to see. A panel-mount switch is easy to secure to the thin wall of a metal lantern housing. Wire together the battery holder, switch, and lamp base. Make it easy to remove so you can switch out batteries and lamps as they die. It is often best if the globe of the lantern is frosted; you will also need to dress the components and wires so they do not cast shadows from the light. If you want your light to flicker like a candle, check out Chapter 9: Smoke and Fire.

Figures 3-5 and 3-6: A 12V A19 lamp will fit the lamp socket and look correct (if the bulb is meant to be visible) but it will not give off the same amount of light as a bulb run from the mains. A 12V halogen is the go-to lamp for bright light from a battery. With an adapter, it can even fit in a screw-in light socket. Plus, it is dimmable just like an incandescent.

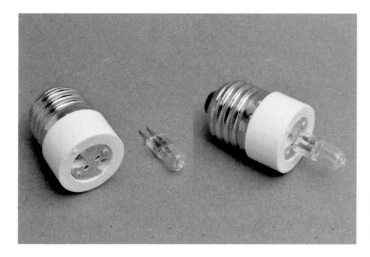 

Figure 3-7: It is handy to keep a number of adapters on hand, like this one that lets you plug a G4 bi-pin lamp into an e26 screw socket. Adapters let you switch what type of bulb you are using without having to rewire the lamp itself.

Figure 3-8: For this lamp, a second socket was attached to the side, and the real socket was disconnected.

LED Lights

Figures 3-9 to 3-11: The LED, battery, and reed switch were small enough to fit inside this actress' mouth. The box contains a magnet which keeps the reed switch in the off position. The actor also had a magnetic ring on his hand. When the light is moved away from the magnet, the reed switch turns the LEDs on. *Love of the Nightingale*, Florida State University, 2015. Photos courtesy of Erin Kehr.

A light-emitting diode (LED) is a small source of light. Their low cost, bright steady light, small power requirement, and lack of heat make them ideal for many prop applications.

We will start with individual LEDs. A few well-placed LEDs can make glowing crystals, indicator lights, fake candles, and other magic and sci-fi elements for under a dollar.

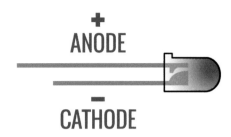

Figure 3-12: The long terminal on the LED is the anode and connects to the positive side of the battery. The short terminal is the cathode and connects to the negative side.

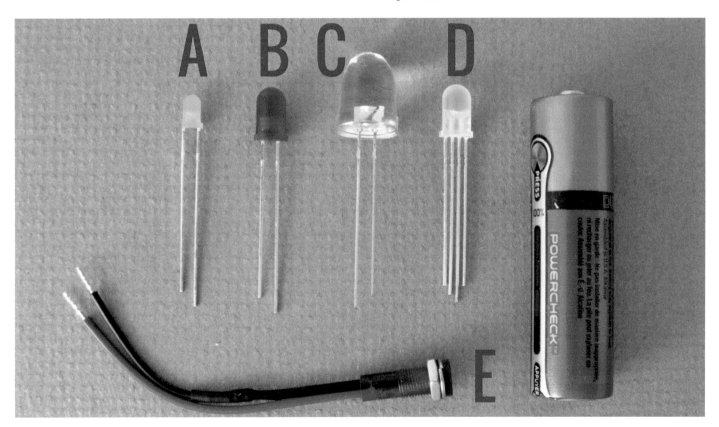

Figure 3-13: Battery for scale. Pictured is a 3mm LED (A), a 5mm LED (B), and a 10mm LED (C). An RGB LED (D) has four terminals, one each for red, blue, and green, and a common cathode. LED assemblies come with a variety of extra parts already attached. This assembly (E) comes with a panel mount and wires, as well as a resistor to make it ready to run on 12V power.

The following shapes and sizes are the most common LEDs you will find:

- 5mm – the old standby. Cheap and common.
- 3mm – smaller. Fits between two pieces of paper. Only shoots from the top, not really from the sides
- 10mm (jumbo) – like small light bulbs. Large and bright, harder to conceal
- Straw hat – wide angle, lots of light from sides, illuminates a large area
- Square – light focused directly out top. Light spread is uneven (prismatic)
- 4 pin – lays flat on a surface. Wider than a 5mm
- Surface Mount – thin and narrow, fits in super tight spaces. Not much light emitted

LEDs and Resistors

Every LED operates within a narrow range of voltage and DC current. With too little voltage, the LED will be very dim or may not illuminate at all. Too much voltage will make the LED burn out quicker; an excessive amount of voltage can kill it almost instantly. You need to calculate precisely how much voltage your LEDs need so you can choose batteries that will provide enough voltage. You will rarely be able to find batteries that provide the exact voltage of your LEDs; instead, you will use batteries that provide more voltage than you need, and then use resistors to reduce the voltage to the exact amount needed.

The voltage used by an LED is known as the **forward voltage**, which is indicated on the LED's datasheet as "Vf." The datasheet is either included with the LED packaging or listed on the website where you order it.

If you do not know the forward voltage of your LEDs, they are pretty standard depending on the color. Typical red, orange, yellow, and yellow-green LEDs have a Vf of 1.8V. Pure Green, blue, white, pink, and UV have a Vf of 3.2V. Most are made to operate under a typical voltage, but the minimum and maximum values can be 0.2 to 0.5V difference.

The LED's datasheet will also indicate which current will give it the longest life (If). Most LEDs operate best at 20 milliamps (mA). Running more current will make it eventually burn out, though intermittent lighting, such as with a blinking LED, will allow it to cool in between and last longer.

When you know the forward voltage of your LED and the current to run it at, you can figure out the resistance needed using Ohm's Law (resistance = voltage/current, or R=V/I). For example, we have an LED with a Vf of 3.2V and we want to run it at 20mA. A standard AA battery only gives us 1.5V, so we use four batteries to give us 6V.

We want the resistor to use a portion of that 6V so that the LED is left with just the 3.2V it needs. If you subtract the two (6V – 3.2V) you find the resistor needs to use 2.8V. Our equation now reads:

$$R = 2.8V / I$$

Next convert the current (20mA) to amps to get I:

$$R = 2.8V / 0.02A$$

This gives us a preferred resistance value of 140Ω.

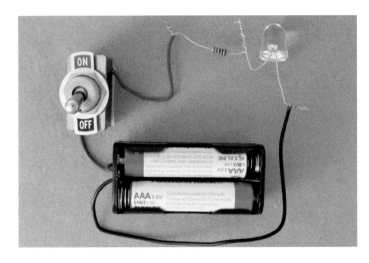

Figure 3-14: Here is our LED wired up to the battery pack, with resistor and switch in place.

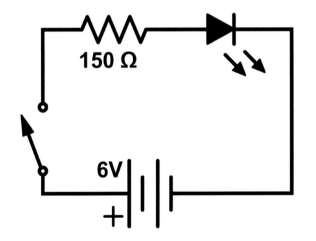

Figure 3-15: Here we have the same circuit represented as a circuit schematic.

You can also use three batteries, which will supply 4.5V, in which case you will use a 68Ω resistor (the next highest resistor to the 65Ω you need). However, battery packs for three batteries are less common.

Resistors come in a variety of values. You can special order a 140Ω resistor, but most sets come with either a 120Ω or a 150Ω. They usually have a tolerance of ±5 (you can find more precise tolerances though). Round up to the next highest value and use the 150Ω.

Multiple LEDs and Resistors

Multiple LEDs can be wired either in parallel or in series. When we run them in parallel, each LED needs its own resistor (wired in series). The resistor value stays the same. The only difference is that the battery will be depleted faster.

If we wire them in series, then we need to recalculate the power requirement and necessary resistance. Four 3.2V LEDs require 12.8V of power. A 9V battery plus four AAs will give us 15V. We still want them to run on 20mA of current.

$$R = (15V - 12.8V) / 0.02A$$
$$R = 2.2V / 0.02A$$
$$R = 110Ω$$

Rounding up to the closest available resistor leaves us choosing the 120Ω.

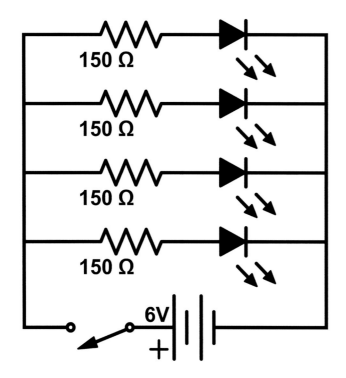

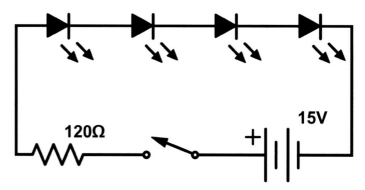

Figure 3-17: Our four LEDs wired in series.

Figure 3-16: Schematic of four 3.2V LEDs run in parallel. Each LED needs a 150Ω resistor just like in our previous example with a single 3.2V LED.

It does not matter whether you attach the resistor to the positive or negative side of the LED. Remember that in series, all components are affected equally regardless of their position. As your circuits get more complex, with multiple paths and branches, then you need to be more careful about your resistor placement, making sure they only affect what you want them to affect and nothing more.

Sometimes, you can get away without needing a resistor. For instance, if you have five LEDs with a forward voltage of 1.8V and you run them in series, they will require 9V. A 9V battery will give you exactly what you need.

You can find LED resistor calculators online. As with any calculator, it is helpful to know how it works and how to find what variables you need and how it all goes together first. Once you understand the whole thing, then a calculator becomes useful. If you are only connecting a few LEDs, it may just be easier to do it by hand.

Miniature Incandescents

Prior to the influx of cheap LEDs, we used miniature incandescent bulbs for the same effects. These are still around, and may come in handy now and then.

Grain of wheat bulbs are tiny incandescent bulbs (about ⅛" diameter) used for model railroads and light-up displays. They have wire leads rather than bases. **Grain of rice** bulbs are even smaller (about ³⁄₃₂" diameter), and are often used as dollhouse lights. **Pea bulbs** are a bit bigger (¼" diameter), and have a screw base.

These are rough definitions, as these naming conventions are not standardized. Though the most common of these bulbs are 12V, they are available anywhere from 1.5V to 16V.

Light Strips

If you want a strip of light rather than a single bulb, you have a number of products to choose from. We will look at LED tape, rope light, EL wire, and other options in the following sections. I will even talk about festoon lighting and Christmas lights, since props people use them for a variety of purposes.

LED Tape

LED tape is a very thin, low-profile, flexible strip of LEDs. The back often has a self-adhesive strip to attach to a surface. It is sometimes called flexible LED strip lights, or even just LED strips, but be aware you can also get rigid LED strips, which may not be what you want.

You can buy LED tape in a variety of lengths, or a whole spool of continuous tape. The tape has marks at regular intervals where you can cut it (which can be every half-inch to every four inches depending on the tape). These marks will run through the middle of soldering pads, so your cut does not disrupt the internal wiring. If you make a cut at any other point, then a few LEDs at that end will not light up, and you will have nowhere to attach your wires.

The end of a spool will usually have a connector or wires already attached, but as you cut pieces off, you will need to attach your own wires or connectors. Wires can either be soldered directly to the end of a length of LED tape, or you can attach a special clip-on connector.

LED tape comes in white, solid colors, or changeable colors. White LED tape comes in a variety of color temperatures; some white LED strips let you control the color temperature.

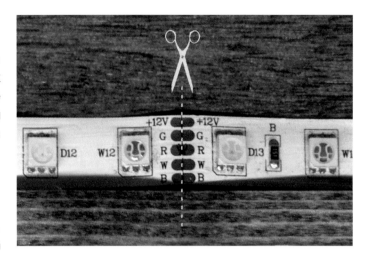

Figure 3-18: Only cut LED tape through the soldering pads, which occur at regular lengths along the LED tape. The pads will also be labeled to help you attach the wires correctly.

Color-changing LED tape comes in RGB, RGBW, RGBA, and more. RGB means you have red, green, and blue LEDs along the whole length. By controlling the brightness of each color, you can mix a number of different, highly saturated colors. RGBW adds in a white LED, giving you the option of mixing more pastel colors or just having a pure white light. RGBA adds amber so you can match incandescent fixtures better and have a warmer light which is more flattering for skin tones. The more colors of LED you have on your tape, the greater range of colors you can mix, though they get more expensive.

If you only need solid colors, you can save money by purchasing a large spool of white LED tape and using colored gels to make whatever color light your prop needs. If you need a lot of LED tape to match, it's best to buy the exact same brand and model; it's even better to buy it all at once, as there can be subtle color variations between different lots of the same tape.

LED tape runs on low voltage, usually 12V or 24V. The power supply will only adequately power a certain length of LED tape. For longer lengths, you need to wire several strips in parallel, or use multiple power sources.

If you simply need to turn the LED tape on and off, you can wire it directly to a power supply. The power supply can then be controlled by wiring in a switch, a remote control, or a DMX controller (see Chapter 11: Control).

If you need to dim your LED tape or change the colors on color-changing tape, you will need a controller in addition to your power supply. Theatrical suppliers sell LED tape that connects to a DMX controller. Consumer brands will come with their own control box or special remote control. Besides dimming and changing colors, some of these controllers let you run flash or chase sequences. For more advanced users, you can hook LED tape up directly to a microcontroller and program it yourself.

Digitally addressable pixel LEDs have controller chips embedded in the actual tape itself, allowing you to control each individual LED from a single input. Some are meant to connect to a microcontroller, which will hold the programming. Others have a DMX input so you can connect it to your light board and program it from there. These allow you to make chases, strobes, and other crazy effects with individual control of each LED. You can even arrange the tape in rows to make a matrix of LEDs, and use pixel-mapping to create simple images.

Figure 3-19: LED tape is made up of individual LEDs which the audience can see if they look directly at it.

Figure 3-20: If you can hide the LED tape, the light will appear as an even glow coming from everywhere. You can also add diffusion over the tape to soften the individual LEDs and make it appear more like a continuous beam of light. *Beautiful Star*, Triad Stage, 2015. Scenic design by Robin Vest; lighting design by Ken White.

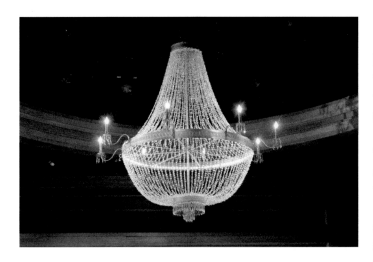

Figure 3-21: LED tape is attached to the inside of the large ring of this chandelier, which caused the crystals to "glow" from the inside. *39 Steps*, Triad Stage, 2014. Scenic design by Timothy Mackabee.

EL Wire

EL wire (Electroluminescent wire) is a wire that glows when current is applied. It is thin and flexible, allowing it to curve around edges or be sewn into fabric. It produces an unbroken line of light, unlike LED tape and tube.

EL wire requires AC power to light up. If you want to run it off batteries, you will need an inverter. EL wire suppliers often include inverter battery packs made just for EL wire.

You can cut EL wire to any length you want. You need to reseal the cut end with hot glue or epoxy to avoid being shocked by the bare wire. This also leaves you with a piece of EL wire without any connectors; soldering a new connector to the end is very tricky, but you can find tutorials online to help you through it.

Rope and Tube Light

Rope light is similar to LED tape except it is encased in a clear plastic tube. Incandescent rope light is one of the ancestors of LED tape; you can still find incandescent rope light as well as LED rope light.

LED tube lights come in a frosted plastic tube, so they appear more like a continuous beam of light from a short distance. Tube lights are a great way to simulate neon signs at a fraction of the cost. As with tape, theatrical suppliers sell LED tube that is easier to integrate with your light board.

Figure 3-22: EL wire powered by a small battery inverter.

Figure 3-23: This "constellation puppet" uses EL wire along the edges and Christmas lights for the stars. *Orphie and the Book of Heroes*, The Kennedy Center, 2014. Photo courtesy of Pam Weiner.

Figure 3-24: Festoon lights. *La Bohème*, Santa Fe Opera, 2007. Set design by Kevin Knight.

A 3V inverter will power about 1 to 15 feet (0.3 to 5m) of typical EL wire, and 1 to 7.5 feet (0.3 to 2.5m) of high-brightness EL wire. A 12V inverter can drive up to 40 feet (12m) of plain wire or 20 feet (6m) of high brightness wire. The longer your EL wire is, the dimmer it will be under a specific voltage. This can get tricky if you have multiple pieces at different lengths which need to match in brightness.

While the brightness of EL wire is roughly determined by its voltage, it cannot be smoothly dimmed from "off" to "full" like incandescents or LEDs. You need a dimmer specifically made for EL wire, like the RC4Magic DMXfb.

Festoon Lighting

Festoon lighting is a chain or string of light bulb bases. You see them outside tents for carnivals and circuses, as well as for weddings and festivals. If you need multiple points of light, they can save you time since they are already wired together and can be powered from a single plug. You can also jumble them up to make a "cloud" of individual light points, or arrange them to make a pattern of lights.

Christmas lights or **garland lights** are smaller strings of lights. Some have the lights hard-wired in, while others have removable bulbs. Traditional Christmas lights use either C7 or C9 incandescent bulbs, while most of the contemporary versions use LEDs in a variety of sizes and shapes.

Other Lighting

Keep your eye out for off-the-shelf light sources you can adapt, such as flashlights, work lights, task lighting, and light-up toys. These will already be wired with a switch and the appropriate power supply, all enclosed within a housing. Auto stores will also have some crazy lighting effects, most made to run off of a 12V battery. Often, these preexisting items are cheaper than buying the comparable components, especially when you find them in secondhand shops and thrift stores.

Dimming

Sometimes you want the ability to dim the lights on your prop. Most often, this is done from the light board, but occasionally you want to control it from the prop itself.

Incandescent and halogen bulbs can be dimmed by adjusting the voltage. A **rheostat** is a variable resistor. If you put one in the circuit, you can dim the lamp by turning the dial; for instance, a 25Ω rheostat goes from 0 to 25Ω. At 0Ω, there is no resistance, so the lamp is as bright as it possibly can be.

It takes some experimentation to find what kind of rheostat will completely dim your bulb. In Thurston James' famous prop book, he found he needed a 30Ω rheostat to completely dim a lamp with 12Ω resistance. Even then, the lamp still drew a small amount of power, draining the battery even when unlit. You can find off-the-shelf controllers to dim your lights more easily.

For AC lamps running on AC power, you can use the household dimmer switches which normally go on the wall. These cannot be used on DC circuits.

LEDs and LED tape cannot be dimmed by adjusting voltage; they use **pulse width modulation** (PWM). You can build and program your own, but it gets tricky at the lower end (from 0 to 10% brightness); the LEDs tend to "pop" on and off, rather than smoothly dimming down to nothing. Cheaper store-bought PWM dimmers will also have this problem. If you buy a controller to dim your LEDs, make sure it compensates for this and smoothly dims all the way from "off" to "full."

Camera Flash

Getting a quick bright flash of light requires a **strobe light**. These can often be expensive, so many props people take apart the camera flash from a disposable camera as a cheap and dirty alternative. These can then be hidden inside vintage camera flash units, gun barrels, or other magic props that require a small flash.

If you break apart the disposable camera body, you should be able to locate the battery, the light, and a small chip that controls the flash. You can also keep the power switch and the camera button itself if you want to avoid wiring your own in.

The flash is powered by a capacitor which draws a large charge from the battery and then discharges it all at once. The main safety concern with this project is that the capacitor can hold a charge *even after the power is turned off and the batteries are removed*. If you touch the leads on a charged capacitor, it will shock you. The voltage is much higher than what the battery outputs; some camera capacitors can go as high as 60V. While unlikely to be lethal, it is certainly harmful and very surprising.

The first thing you want to do when you open the camera case is to bridge the two leads with an insulated screwdriver to discharge the capacitor. This should create a bright arc, but if your screwdriver is adequately insulated, you will not feel anything. The capacitor is now safe to touch until you charge it back up. For extra safety, you can cover the leads with heat-shrink tube to insulate them.

Diffusion and Color

Diffusion means spreading the light out so it shines more evenly. It is useful for concealing the individual sources of light or for casting light with softer edges.

Your electrics department has sheets of diffusion material for their own lights which you might be allowed to borrow. Any translucent plastic or fabric will help diffuse the light. The more diffusion you add, the dimmer your light will be.

With clear plastic or glass, you can spray on a frosted coating or a light layer of spray paint. With plastic, you can sand the surface to help it catch the light.

You can use similar techniques to change the color of your light. Again, your lighting friends should have all sorts of colors of gel. Multiple layers of gel and/or diffusion can help achieve more precise effects.

If you hide a light behind or inside a transparent or translucent prop (such as one cast in plastic), you can make it glow even if the exterior is painted to look solid. It is similar to a painted scrim which appears solid when lit from the front, but disappears when lit from behind. It needs to be relatively dark for this trick to be effective.

Figure 3-25: Sanding the outside of these acrylic icicles helps catch the light from LEDs stuck in their bases. *Snow Queen*, Riverside Children's Theater, 2015. Photos courtesy of Kylie Clark.

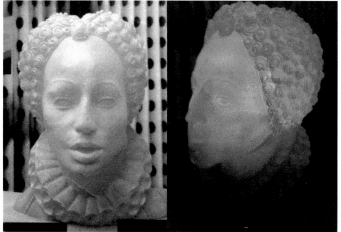

Figure 3-26: This bust of Mary Stuart was cast in clear resin with lights inserted inside. The outside was painted to look like white marble, but when the lights turned on, the whole thing glowed. *Molly's Veil*, Prairie Theatre Exchange, 2005. Set design by Carole Klemm, prop made by Larry Demedash, photos courtesy of Kari Hagness.

Lightboxes

A **lightbox** makes a surface glow with a uniform light. In theatre, we often want a lightbox to simulate a moon, to fake the front of a TV screen, or to backlight a poster, though there are many other uses for it.

To get an evenly lit surface, the surface needs to be translucent. Additional diffusion can be added behind the surface or on the lights themselves. If the inside of the box is white, the light will bounce around more; it may even be possible to illuminate the surface entirely with the bounce, and avoiding having lights shine directly on it. For more even illumination, use multiple light sources and place them as far from the surface as possible.

If you cannot afford the real estate to make a lightbox, you have a few options for thin, light-up panels. EL panels, like EL wire, provide a continuous, flexible surface of light. They are expensive though: a panel the size of a sheet of paper will run you nearly $50.

The Rosco LitePad uses LEDs to illuminate a thin, non-flexible panel. It comes in a variety of sizes, making it useful to fake a smartphone screen or even a laptop screen.

four

motion

This chapter talks about two different kinds of motion: moving a prop around stage, and building a prop with moving parts. First we will look at moving a prop around stage, whether that means pushing it on, tracking it across, or flying it in.

Moving on and off Stage

One of the most common tasks for a props department is adding casters or glides to furniture and large props so they can be moved quickly during scene changes. In a director's ideal world, a chair will slide onto the stage effortlessly and quietly, and then stay perfectly still during the scene. Despite decades of research and development, we still do not have the perfect solution for this. You will need to compromise and accept one or more of these realities: seeing the casters or other mechanism, hearing some noise while moving, watching the crew activate the brakes or drop a pin, using a lot of strength to move, or spending a whole lot of money.

To get larger props on and off stage, they will need casters, glides, or some kind of moving platform (either a wagon or skid).

Casters

A **caster** is a wheel you can mount to your prop. The two main types are rigid (or straight) and swivel. A rigid caster will only move in a straight line, while a swivel caster will turn to move in whichever direction you want.

Swivel casters have a certain amount of "throw" to them; when you make an abrupt change in direction, the prop will have a bit of side-to-side movement as the caster corrects itself. A **triple-swivel caster** has three swivel casters mounted to a rotating plate in order to

give you "zero throw." A **ball caster** seems like the dream solution for a low-profile caster with zero throw. However, ball casters are designed for facing up, and using them as casters results in horrific noise. The ones that can actually be used face down as casters are just as tall as regular casters.

The mounting for a caster can be either a plate or a stem. **Plate casters** are the easiest to mount: you simply screw or bolt them to the bottom of your prop. Some plate casters are made to attach to the side as well. A **stem caster** feeds into a hole. The stem can either be threaded like a bolt or be held in place by friction. Stem casters are useful for the bottoms of furniture legs which lack anywhere to mount a plate and where a plate would stick out.

The material composition of the wheel will give your caster different properties. Rubber is soft, cushioning, and very quiet. However, it can mark certain floor

Figure 4-1: On top: A swivel caster and a rigid caster, both with plates. On bottom: A stem caster.

surfaces and can wear down or even break apart. Plastic wheels, whether polyurethane, nylon, or phenolic, are a lot harder, abrasion resistant, and non-marking. They are also louder on hard surfaces.

Metal wheels can carry much heavier weights, probably far greater than props will need. They also leave marks on many surfaces. Wooden wheels can only carry lighter loads, but they are more historically accurate for period props.

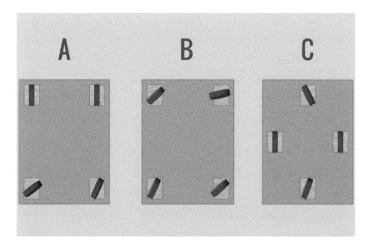

Figure 4-2: A) With two swivel casters in the rear and two rigid in the front, you can easily move in a straight line but turn when needed. However, you need space to turn. With brakes only on the swivel side, the whole thing becomes immobile. B) Four swivel casters make it easy to spin and maneuver in tight spaces (like a furniture dolly). When moving, it can be hard to change direction, especially with heavier pieces. C) Placing the casters in a diamond pattern with swivels in front and back and rigids on the side makes it as easy to maneuver as A but allows you to pivot in place. This pattern can be unstable and noisy though, so is usually only good for backstage.

Caster Placement

We rarely want to see the casters. For a piece of furniture with a closed bottom, they can be placed inside and hidden by the skirt or apron. While it is tempting to have the furniture ride as low as possible, you should leave a gap of at least ½″ (12.5 mm) between the floor and the lowest point of the prop. Anything less is likely to rub against a slightly uneven floor or get caught when going over small obstructions.

When attaching swivel casters on the inside of a prop, be sure to leave room on all sides so the caster is free to swivel all the way around.

Wheels and Axles

When a two-wheeled wagon or cart turns, the wheels spin at different speeds. If the wheels are both fixed to the same axle, it won't be able to turn.

Figure 4-3: A two-wheeled cart with a split axle.

Glides and Slides

Glides or slides let you move props and furniture without adding extra height, as often happens with casters. They are also handy if you need to avoid wheels for aesthetic reasons. The prop is more likely to stay in place without needing to lock any wheels. The trade-off is that you need continuous effort when pushing, unlike wheels which have momentum once the prop starts moving.

The material you choose for your glide ultimately depends on what type of surface you are pushing over. Generally, you use hard plastics when pushing over carpet or heavily textured floors (including expanded steel), and you use felt or fabric when pushing over hard or slick floors. Be ready to try a few options, particularly when your floor is made of unconventional materials or if you need to push over multiple types of surfaces.

Furniture glides are made from any number of hard plastics. Some have holes for screwing on, others have an attached threaded rod for bolting on. Some have a "cup" shape meant to hold a furniture leg, while others have a self-adhesive backing. The "cup" versions will not stay put if the furniture is lifted, and the self-adhesive ones frequently come off under normal theatrical use.

Ultra-high-molecular-weight polyethylene (UHMW) is as slick as Teflon, but holds up better to wear and tear. It comes in sheets and bars which are easy to cut into custom glides for the bottom of heavy props and furniture. You can drill and countersink screw holes for sturdy attachment. Be sure to countersink far enough that the screw head does not rub against the floor. Also, you can round over the edges so it is less likely to catch on any seams or cracks in the floor.

Felt is almost always glued on. This can make it very easy to tear off, especially with heavy use. Screwing or stapling it on the bottom is not recommended since the floor will get scratched up. Whenever possible, wrap the felt around two or more sides of a foot and staple or screw it in there. Pieces of carpet can also be used as glides. Experiment with different kinds of felt and carpet to see which moves best over the surfaces of your set.

Wagons and Skids

A **wagon** is a small platform on casters which carries furniture. It can carry a single prop or a small arrangement of furniture for a scene.

A **skid** is a low-profile platform without casters. It is usually just a sheet of plywood with glides that is "skidded" across the stage.

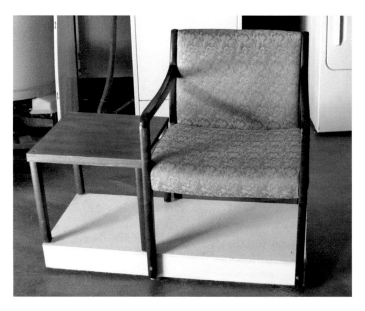

Figure 4-4: This table and chair were attached to a single wagon on glides so they could be pushed into place quickly by a single crew member. *Wit*, Triad Stage, 2014. Designed by Fred Kinney.

For wagons and skids, the prop may be attached to the platform, or it may just need to be steady enough to get on stage, where it is then picked up and moved around by the actors. They can be pushed on with poles or pulled on by strings and cables. They can also be on a track with a winch or automation. When tracks are involved, it is more likely to be the responsibility of scenery. Larger wagons and skids, or wagons which carry scenic elements as well as props, are often scenery's purview as well.

Always push and pull the wagon, not the furniture.

Figure 4-5: This push stick has holes which fit over pins on this low-profile skid, making it secure while pushing but easily removable when the scene starts. *Cendrillon*, Santa Fe Opera, 2006.

Figures 4-6 and 4-7: This large hedge rolled on from stage left. Its length made it difficult to steer when pushed from the end. The solution was to hide a crew person inside to "Flintstone" it. *Don Giovanni*, Santa Fe Opera, 2004. Scenic design by David Zinn. Photo courtesy of Andreea Mincic.

Figure 4-8: Two wheels pointed toward each other at a 45° angle can ride along a single piece of angle iron. Skate wheels or bearings are small but strong. This is a useful way to make a track when you do not have a lot of depth.

Figure 4-9: Wagon brakes require a place on your prop to mount, and if visible to the audience, they can be quite ugly and distracting.

Preventing Wheels from Moving

Of course, directors do not just want wheeled props that can move quickly and quietly during transitions. They also want them to hold their position during the scene, no matter how hard actors interact with them. We have a number of methods to accomplish this, each with their own advantages and disadvantages. What you choose depends on the specific circumstances of the scene shift, the size and shape of your prop, your resources and capabilities, and various other factors.

Some casters have locks on them. A **locking caster** is useful because you do not need to further modify the prop or set to hold it in position. These have a disadvantage for *a vista* scene changes because the audience has to watch a crew member walk around to each caster, bend over, and lock it (though some can be locked using your feet). You also need to be able to reach the lock, meaning the casters may remain visible. You can solve this by using a fabric apron to hide them.

A **wedge** acts like a doorstop on your prop. Like a locking caster, you need to watch a crew person bend over and put each one in during the scene shift; they need to be placed on each side to keep it from moving in any direction. They may not be the most secure locking mechanism depending on the surface of your stage. They also only work on wagons or boxy props: you cannot use them on chairs or other props with tall legs.

A **wagon brake**, sometimes called a toggle clamp or Destaco (a popular brand name), is positioned so it lifts the prop off its casters when engaged. You often only need two brakes to keep a prop from moving, and they can sometimes be operated by foot, making them a

Figures 4-10 and 4-11: A cane bolt goes through a hole in the wagon and a hole in the deck.

more elegant choice when the audience is watching the scene shift.

Barrel bolts and **cane bolts** can be added to your prop so that they slide into a hole in the stage to hold them in place. Unlike the previously mentioned braking mechanisms, bolts require you to drill a hole into the stage. This is not always possible or allowed, depending on the set. This also means the positions of the props need to be determined beforehand, and changing their location during tech requires a new hole to be drilled and the old one filled. Also, if the crew cannot easily line the prop up with the hole, they will be unable to drop the bolt and the prop will not be locked in place. However, they are a very secure locking method, and it is easier to hide their appearance than the other methods.

You can also have a foot iron which either hinges or slides down to the ground. A set screw passes through a hole in the iron and screws into the floor. This is accomplished by drilling a threaded insert into the stage floor. This offers the same disadvantages as a bolt, but gives a very secure connection.

With a lift jack, the casters are on a hinged plate which allows the prop to sit on its legs while onstage, and then lift onto the wheels to move it. This is a great mechanism if you have the resources to fabricate it and if the prop is large enough to allow it.

Air-lift casters use pneumatic power to lift a single caster. You can find a few commercially available versions, though they are more popular as a shop-built project.

Tracking in and on

For larger props that track on and off from above, the track is often hung by scenery. Smaller props can have simpler tracking systems.

Figures 4-12 and 4-13: The casters are on a plate which hinges out of the way so the prop can rest on its legs. When the side of the prop is lifted, the plate swings down; with a smooth enough motion, the crew person can lift the prop, let the plate swing down, then set it onto the wheels before the plate swings back.

Figures 4-14 and 4-15: A pneumatic cylinder pushes the lift jack so this unit can roll. When the cylinder retracts, gravity lowers the unit onto its legs. This allows the entire prop to become mobile or immobile just by the flick of a switch in the back. *Sherlock Holmes: The Final Adventure*, Actors Theatre of Louisville, 2006.

A curtain track is a useful solution for lightweight props. Some track systems allow you to attach multiple pieces together to make track as long as you need it. They may also have curved pieces that allow you to change direction.

A more homemade version (also used by curtains) is a rod that you slide rings along. Your prop hangs from the rings. The length is limited by where you have to hang the rod from, since the rings can't travel past these hanging points.

Rolling Objects

Sometimes your show calls for props that roll around stage, such as cannonballs and oranges. Insert a weight in one side to make it off balance. If hollow, fill it with a bit of weight on one side. The off-balance weight will help it settle more quickly and keep it from rolling uncontrollably into the audience.

Props with Moving Parts

Now we get to the second half of our chapter, where we look at props that have moving parts. Most moving parts can be categorized according to three major actions: hinge, rotate, and slide. We will look at each in turn.

Hinges

A hinge, or a pivot joint, can be as simple as attaching an actual hinge to two pieces. You can make your own pivots by running a pin or shaft through holes in two or more pieces of material. A cloth center-hinge is a third way of hinging materials; glue a piece of cloth to two boards to make a "flap." A thin width of cloth allows the hinge

You do not need to fabricate all your moving parts from scratch. You can find lots of mechanisms all around you, ready to be adapted into props. Mechanical and electrical toys are particularly fruitful sources. Also look at VCRs, CD players, automobile parts (like windshield wipers and power windows), holiday decorations, infant swings, oscillating fans, and more. If you buy these items at thrift stores and flea markets, you can pick up completed mechanisms for a fraction of the cost of the individual components.

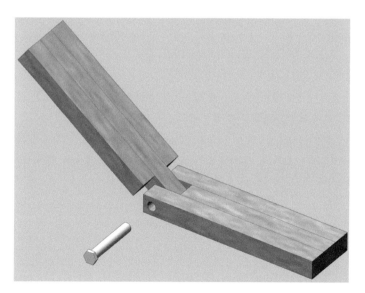

Figure 4-16: When fabricating your own hinge joints, sandwich one side between two pieces on the other side. This helps keep the pin perpendicular. If you are using a nut and bolt as your pin, it also prevents the nut from working itself loose.

to have some side-to-side movement. Using a rope or cord as the hinge gives the greatest amount of freedom, resulting in a hinge that can bend in any direction.

For a pinned joint, you need a pin that will not work its way loose. A nut and bolt is the easiest and most readily available type of pin. It is better if the parts rotate on the solid part of the bolt rather than the threads, as they are weaker and you can wear the threads away through too much rubbing. You also want to avoid having the rotating part rub against the nut since it can turn itself loose over time.

Linkages

When you have multiple bars or rods connected by hinges or pivot points, you have a **linkage**. A linkage can give you complicated motion just by rotating one of the pivot points or moving one of the bars back and forth.

One common type of linkage is the **four bar mechanism**.

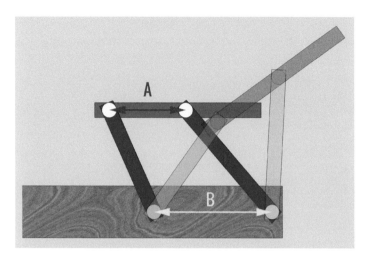

Figure 4-18: Adjusting the distance between the pivots on the green bar and the base (A and B) will cause the green bar to swing as it moves. Adjusting just the lengths of the arms (C and D) will give the green bar a nearly constant tilt throughout its movement. Adjust both the pivots and the arms for further variations in movement.

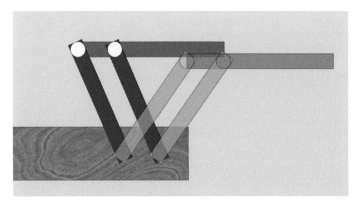

Figure 4-17: In a four bar mechanism, two arms (blue) pivot a third bar (green). When the arms are the same length and the pivot points on the green bar and wood bar are equidistant, then the green bar will remain parallel to the wood bar as it swings.

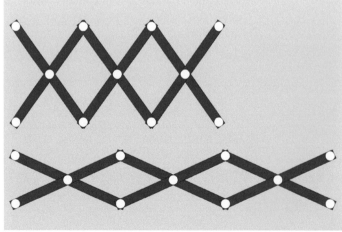

Figure 4-19: A scissors mechanism.

Another useful linkage is the **scissors mechanism**. This provides a lot of linear motion with only a little amount of pushing.

Levers

Since hinge joints can act as levers, knowing the principles of leverage will help you design more effective hinge joints and linkages.

The lever shown below is an example of a first-class lever. The fulcrum is in the middle of the two weights or forces. First-class levers include crowbars and scissors. This type of lever is useful when you need to change the direction of your force, such as when you want to push down to make an object go up.

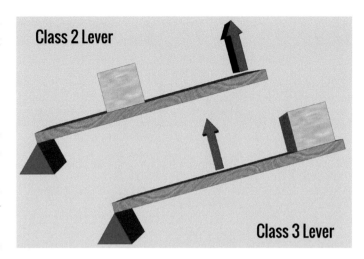

Figure 4-21: In a second-class lever, you apply force on the same side of the fulcrum as the weight. Examples include wheelbarrows, nutcrackers, and bottle openers. With a third-class lever, you apply force in the middle of the bar. Examples include tongs, golf clubs, and fishing rods.

The "weight" is actually a force. A stationary object's weight is equal to its mass times the acceleration due to gravity. There's a lot of physics, which most props people can usually ignore. However, you do need to keep in mind the effects of gravity. Also, keep in mind the weight of the lever parts themselves.

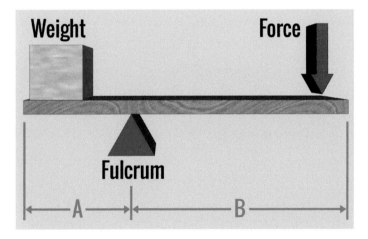

Figure 4-20: In this lever, B is twice as far from the fulcrum as A. You only need to apply half as much force as the object weights. However, you need to move that side of the lever twice as far as the weight will move. Every lever has a simple ratio like that; it is balanced when the force times the distance to the fulcrum on one side is equal to the force times the distance to the fulcrum on the other, or $F_1 \times d_1 = F_2 \times d_2$.

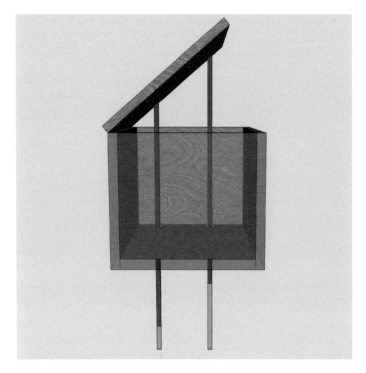

Figure 4-23: Bearings come in a plethora of mounting options. A commonly used one in theatre is a pillow block, which is a bearing that mounts to a base or another surface.

Figure 4-22: In this ultra-simplified example of a box, the lid is magically opened by pushing a bar which extends from the floor. The lid acts as a class 3 lever, and its own weight is the force you need to lift. Look how the placement of the push bar changes things. The red bar does not need to move as far as the blue bar, but you need to exert a lot more force to lift the lid.

Rotation

The simplest kind of rotation can be accomplished by drilling a hole and sliding a cylinder into it. For rapid or precise rotation, the friction of a rod in a hole might be too much. To reduce friction, you can use either bushings or bearings. A **bushing** is a small sleeve that goes around the rod and fits into the hole. It is either made of a material with low friction or it has some built-

in lubrication. A flanged bushing has a flange to keep it from falling out of the hole.

A **bearing** uses small balls (ball bearings) to keep all points of contact to a minimum.

Shafts

Nearly anything cylindrical can be used for rotation. You can use a rod made of metal, plastic, or wood (wood rods are also called "dowels"). Bolts and nails can be used as well. Regular rods of material may not be smoothly finished or precisely measured. A proper **shaft** is a rod with properties that make it ideal for rapid rotation. Some shafts are **keyed**, meaning they have a groove or flat area running the length of it. This makes it easier

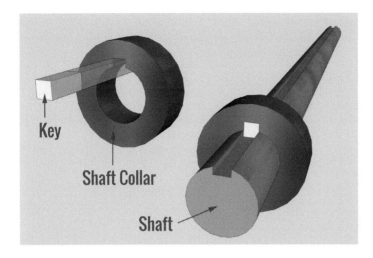

Figure 4-24: A key is a small bar of metal that fits in the keyway (slot) of both the shaft and the component being connected to the shaft.

Figure 4-26: This motor and gearbox has a shaft coupler attached.

to firmly attach other components and keep them from spinning independently of the shaft.

Shaft **couplings** allow you to attach two shafts together, while **shaft adapters** let you attach two shafts of different diameters together. A shaft **collar** is added to hold components in place, or to keep the shaft itself from sliding out of its hole. Couplings, adapters, and collars typically use set screws to hold them to the shaft, and they may also be keyed for a more secure hold. Sometimes the hardest part about connecting things to a crank or motor is finding the right pieces to fit on the shaft.

Cranks

A hand-powered crank can be used to turn a shaft. A **crank** is an arm which sticks out perpendicularly to a rotating shaft (you can also use a full disc instead of just an arm). The farther the crank handle is from the shaft,

Figure 4-25: For this wooden gear, a thin dowel was inserted through the wooden shaft, and the gear had a slot to fit over it. This ensured the gear could not spin independently of the shaft.

the less force you have to apply to turn it, but your hand has to move a further distance to make one rotation. It also makes it easier on the body, because turning a crank with your arm and hand uses stronger muscles than trying to spin a shaft with your fingers.

Motors

Electric motors are used to spin a shaft when you need a greater speed or more power than can be achieved by hand. They are also used to make a prop spin "magically," or when you simply do not have a crew member available to turn a crank. Motors come in a virtually unlimited array of sizes, speeds, and power. You can shop for them, or salvage them from any number of devices.

Speed is measured in revolutions per minute, or RPM. The standard tiny DC hobby motor can have a speed around 10,000 RPM, while a clock motor has an obvious speed of 1 RPM. You can use gears, belts, or chains to reduce the speed by half, a third, or even by ten, but you can keep your prop simpler by using a motor that already spins at the speed you need. A **gearbox** will change the RPM of a motor; some motors come with gearboxes attached (either externally or internally), while other gearboxes are made to attach to existing motors.

AC and DC motors are different and you typically cannot run an AC motor on DC power, or vice versa. If the device runs off of batteries, it is a DC motor. If the device has to plug in (it does not have an internal battery) and the cord does not have a wall wart or transformer anywhere, it is likely an AC motor. Some motors can be powered by either AC or DC, while others may appear to work for a while using the wrong electricity, but will eventually fail.

Figure 4-27: Here is a motor scrounged from a sewing machine alongside a standard 130 size DC hobby motor. The sewing machine motor already has a belt pulley attached to the shaft.

DC motors can be pulled from toys with wheels, cordless drills and other tools, computer fans, electric toothbrushes and razors, cassette players, and automobile starter motors. AC motors can be pulled from vacuum cleaners, sewing machines, blenders, ceiling fans, and record players.

The **torque** of a motor is the strength of its rotation. A computer fan will stop with the slightest touch from your finger, while a ceiling fan is strong enough to spin the attached fan blades.

Look at how the motor is controlled too, as you can use those parts as well. For instance, a cordless drill can spin at several different speeds and has a switch to change directions.

You will also need to mount your motor and attach the shaft to the parts you want to spin. Smaller motors can be secured with zip ties or hose clamps. Larger motors often have holes for bolts.

Figure 4-28: The motor and wheels of a toy car are used to turn this loop of canvas for a player piano. Photo courtesy of Patrick Drone.

Figure 4-29: A timing belt has teeth so it will not slip like a normal belt, and it is quieter than a chain. Here, a series of timing belts and pulleys spin four shafts simultaneously at the same speed.

If you want to attach the motor directly to your shaft, you may need a combination of shaft collars and shaft adapters to do it. You can also use an offset connection, where the motor spins the shaft using either a pulley or a sprocket. A pulley is used with a belt, while a **sprocket** is like a toothed pulley used to move a chain.

Servos

A **servo motor** is meant to rotate to a specific position rather than spinning around continuously. It spins at a very low speed but with a lot of torque. When given a command, it rotates to its position then holds it there until it receives another command. Most kinds of hobby servos cannot spin all the way around, just back and forth within a semicircle. This makes them great for small amounts of motion, such as opening and closing a box, or turning a head back and forth. They typically operate between 4.5V and 6V.

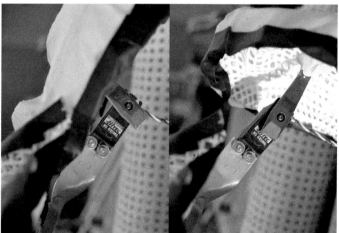

Figure 4-30: This servo makes a puppet's mouth open and close.

You need a controller with your servo. Stores for robotics will sell a variety of control boxes that connect directly to one or more servos and control them using either dials or joysticks. RC shops will carry transmitters and receivers for controlling multiple servos, again using joysticks or dials. Most microcontrollers can be programmed to manipulate servos, which gives you the freedom of having them run automatically, in response to sensors, or in a programmed sequence that relies on the timing and positioning of other moving parts.

A **positional rotation servo** rotates within a 180-degree range, but cannot turn beyond that. A **continuous rotation servo** can turn in any direction independently and continuously.

Most of the hobby servos used in props are positional rotation servos. The cheap servos often have problems at the far ends of their rotation (such as stuttering or getting stuck), so their usable range is slightly less than 180 degrees.

Servos can be either analog or digital. They look the same, but process information differently. Analog servos are essentially "off" until you transmit an action. This gives them a sluggish reaction time on their initial start. Digital servos have quicker and smoother response times, but use more power since they are "on" continuously.

Sliding

Sliding gives you linear motion. The most low-tech method to make a piece slide is by pushing or pulling. You can use a string to pull. With a pulley on the other end, you can use a string to push and pull. A push rod is used when you can't have a pulley on the other end. A push rod will not stretch like a string either. However, a string can go around bends and corners using pulleys or eye bolts to change its path.

Figures 4-31 and 4-32: This crow's head turns by using an aluminum push rod connected to a pivoting control stick. String was too stretchy to allow instantaneous and precise movement. *Snow Queen*, Triad Stage, 2013. Puppet design by Bill Brewer.

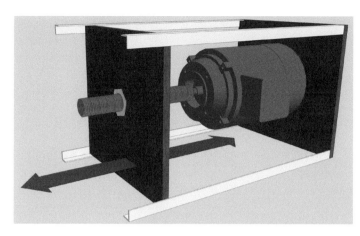

Figure 4-33: This nut is embedded in a piece of wood on a track so it cannot spin around. When the motor spins the threaded rod, the wood moves back and forth. Even when the motor spins very quickly, it still translates into a fairly slow linear motion.

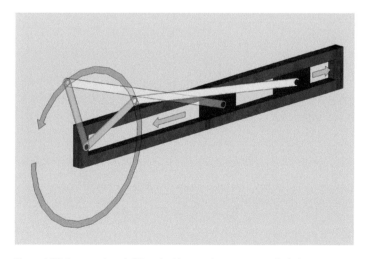

Figure 4-34: In a crank and slider, the blue crank rotates on a shaft. It connects to the yellow arm via a pivot, which is connected to the red block via another pivot. The red block will move back and forth in a linear path as long as it is confined to a track.

A **linear actuator** is a mechanism which creates linear motion. Most will only create a finite amount of travel between two points (usually just a few centimeters or inches). Two types commonly used in props are linear servos and pneumatic cylinders.

A **linear servo** is an electromechanical linear actuator and is sometimes referred to as a linear actuator (though it is only one type of linear actuator). It typically contains a threaded rod and a nut; when one of them spins, the nut travels back and forth along the rod.

You can build your own linear actuator by attaching a threaded rod to the shaft of a motor. Add a nut to the rod. The nut must be free to move back and forth but needs to be kept from spinning with the rod.

Pneumatic cylinders use pressurized air inside a cylinder to either push or pull a rod. They will be covered in great detail in Chapter 6: Pneumatics. One advantage over motors and other electrical components is they can hold their position and carry weight without needing additional power.

An electromechanical **solenoid** is an electric coil that moves a steel plunger when it is energized. Each solenoid is designed to either push or pull; some plungers have a spring so they return to their original position when the energy is turned off. Since the movement is very jerky and fairly instantaneous, solenoids are more often used as triggers than for linear motion, and they will be covered in more detail in Chapter 5: Trick Mechanisms.

A **crank and slider** is another mechanism you can fabricate. A rod is attached to the end of the crank, which pushes a block back and forth.

A winch or drum pulls a string or cable as you turn a crank, wrapping it up along the shaft. If you are moving objects vertically, then a winch can pull them up and use gravity to lower them down.

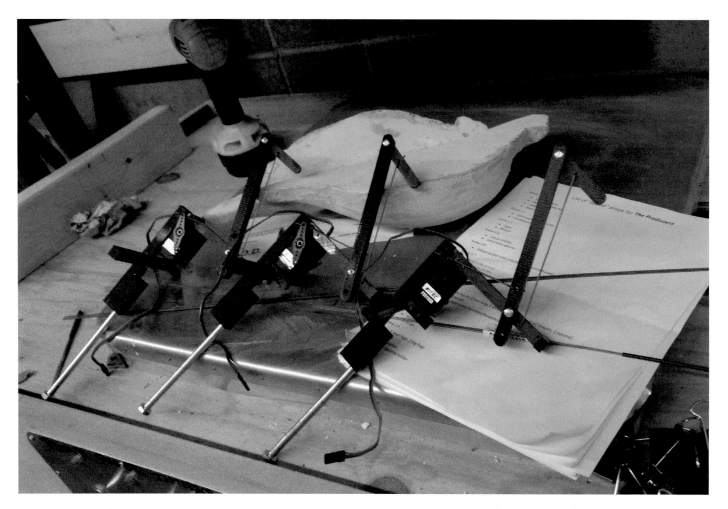

Figure 4-35: These animatronic pigeons use a combination of all types of joint motion. A servo motor rotates to pull and push a rod which is attached to a pivoting bar. *The Producers*, Omaha Community Playhouse, 2016. Photo courtesy of Darin Kuehler.

five

trick mechanisms

This chapter is all about adapting your props to perform tricks which they would not normally perform in real life.

Trick Line

The definition of **trick line** depends on who you ask. In general, it is a smooth, black, non-stretch cord meant to be invisible on stage and is used for doing tricks. It can move props, swing levers, pull pins, or otherwise trigger effects. It may run offstage through pulleys until it reaches a crew member who can operate it.

A theatrical supplier may have a specific product which they call trick line. Some places consider trick line and tie line to be interchangeable. **Tie line** is generally unrated ⅛" diameter black cord with a braided sleeve around a core. You most often find it with electricians who use it to tie cables up to pipes.

General suppliers may not know the term but still have cords which can be used as trick line. Black **mason line** is often used. You want a soft, uncoated cord to make it easy to go through pulleys and around bends, and easy to tie and hold knots. It should be strong. The size depends on what you are doing; ⅛" diameter is great for triggering many prop effects, while ¼" or even ½" may be necessary when hoisting a lot of weight.

Paracord is handy for trick line because it is designed to hold a lot of weight and is readily available in many types of stores.

Fishing line is the thinnest and least visible type of trick line. It comes in two main types: monofilament and braided. Monofilament is often made of clear nylon, while braided is black. What you use depends on the lighting and background. Monofilament is transparent, but can be shiny if it catches a bit of light. Braided line is dark and matte, but it may be visible in front of very light surfaces and areas. Some people call black braided fishing line "spider wire," based on one of the more popular brands.

A load **rating** is how much weight a piece of rigging can safely support, such as a rope, cable, chain, shackle, or hook. Rated materials will specify how much weight they have been engineered to hold. Unrated materials may support some weight, but the amount has never been tested, and it may not be consistent; one unrated shackle may hold 50 pounds without breaking, while another snaps in half when loaded with 30 pounds.

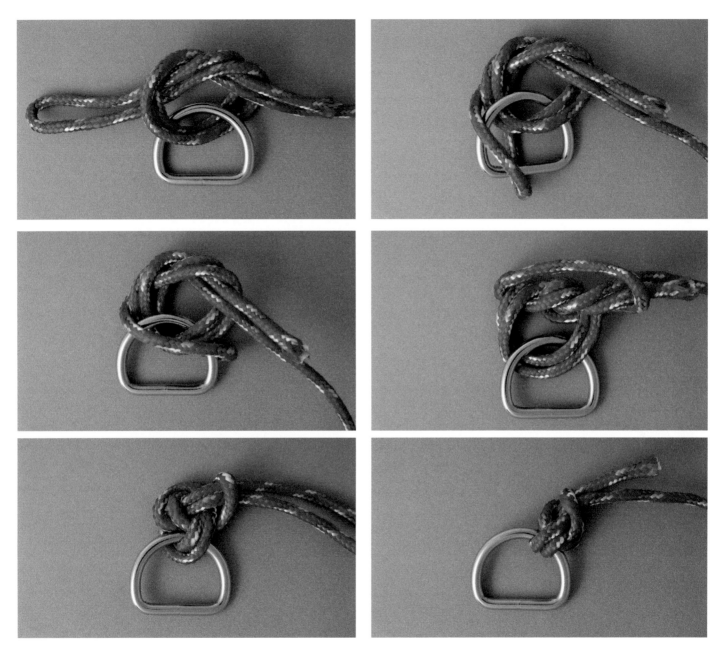

Figures 5-1 to 5-6: Many regular knots will slip when tied in monofilament; use fishing knots instead. One popular strong knot is the Palomar knot, shown here in red line for clarity. Double up the line and make an overhead knot through the ring of what you are tying to. Pass the loop around the ring back up to the knot. Pull everything tight.

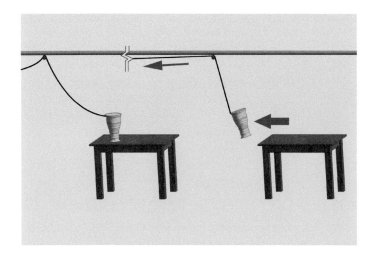

Figure 5-7: A trick line which rises diagonally from an object to a pulley will cause the object to swing in a long pendulum path when the line is pulled tight.

Tricks with Trick Line

> One piece of string is worth a stage full of sophisticated machinery and if it does fail, it is easy to put right.
> Roger Oldhamstead, *Theatre Props*, 1975.

You can find so many tricks to accomplish with trick line. Tie it to a prop that needs to be knocked over by a ghost or a bullet, and it can be jerked from offstage. The line can pass through a small hole in the scenery or furniture. Attach it to a small door that needs to magically open. Use it to make props float and fly upwards.

Flying In and Out

Though the rigging of flying props is often handled by the carpenter or fly rail operator, a props person occasionally hangs a pulley or two for smaller tricks. Depending on

the venue, the props department may not be permitted to hang things: always check first.

If your prop hangs from a single string, it will likely spin in place and swing back and forth. Hanging it from

Figure 5-8: With a single pulley, you are changing the direction. The amount of force it takes to move the object is equal to its weight.

Figure 5-9: Two pulleys will keep the prop from spinning.

Figure 5-10: A double pulley means you have to apply half the force to lift the prop, but you have to pull the lift line twice as far as you want the prop to move. This setup will also keep the prop from spinning if you cannot use two pulleys from the grid.

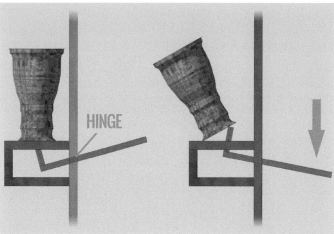

Figure 5-11: A rod on a lever, hidden inside a shelf, can be pushed from behind the wall to knock a knick-knack off the shelf.

two lines will stop the spinning but not the swinging. Three lines will keep it steady. Multiple pulleys on a single line give you a mechanical advantage when lifting.

A **barrel swivel** is used in fishing to keep the line from spinning. As ropes pass through pulleys, they twist and cause the whole line to spin; attach a barrel swivel between the rope and the prop to prevent this.

Gravity Tricks

Many tricks can be accomplished by removing a pin which is holding or supporting something and allowing gravity to take over. The pins can be attached to trick line to allow an offstage crew member to pull them. Multiple trick lines can be run offstage to a single location for a choreographed scene of property destruction.

Figure 5-12: One side of this shelf is held up with a removable pin. The other side is held with a fixed support that allows the shelf to rotate freely. Pulling the pin causes the shelf to swing down and everything on it to slide off.

Kabuki Drops

One of the most iconic gravity tricks in theatre is the kabuki drop. A **kabuki drop** is a thin, lightweight drop automatically released from above the stage. It can be either a curtain which appears from nowhere, unfurling from the sky, or it can be a hanging curtain which is released and flutters to the ground. A double kabuki drop will accomplish both: first a curtain appears out of nowhere, then it falls to the ground.

Though the scenery department handles large-scale kabuki drops, the mechanism is useful for props people in designing similar smaller-scale effects. A batten holding the curtain will have two rings side by side. A ring on the curtain goes between those two rings. A pin goes through all three rings to hold the curtain up. When the pin is pulled, the curtain drops.

A curtain hangs from several points along a batten, so each point will have its own mechanism. The individual pins can be ganged together with string or a stiff rod to pull them all simultaneously. A powerful solenoid can also pull all of them at once, or individual solenoids can be placed at each pin.

For a double kabuki drop, the drop is held in a fabric cradle which is held on one end by kabuki mechanisms. When the pins for the cradle are released, the drop unfurls from above and hangs in view. A second set of kabuki mechanisms holds the drop itself; it can fall to the floor on a subsequent cue.

You can use a fabric cradle with kabuki mechanisms to hold anything that needs to drop, like a bunch of banana peels or a stuffed doll.

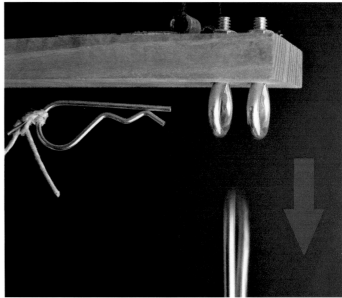

Figures 5-13 and 5-14: A single kabuki drop mechanism in action.

Pins

You can make your own pins with a piece of metal rod. Drill a small hole to tie a piece of trick line to the end, or weld a ring on. A large nail can be used as a pin; dull the end down first. The tapered end makes it easier to guide into a hole. Any kind of smooth pin with a head, like a clevis pin, is useful. The pins from loose-pin hinges are handy to use if your shop already has them lying around.

An **R-clip**, sometimes known as a **spring cotter pin** or **hitch pin**, is a double-pronged pin with one pin bent in a wavy pattern, very much like a bobby pin. The shape allows it to stay in place but still be removable with a hard-enough pull.

A **quick-release pin** has a small ball bearing which protrudes at the end to hold the pin in place. A small spring is behind the ball, so if you pull the pin hard enough, the ball will retract into the pin. Some versions have a button at the end you can push to retract the ball.

These pins require a very precise hole that is bigger than the pin but small enough for the ball bearing to catch.

A **barrel bolt** is a great mechanism for a retractable pin that remains in place.

Solenoids

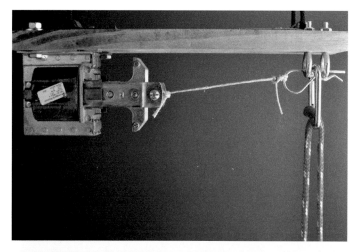

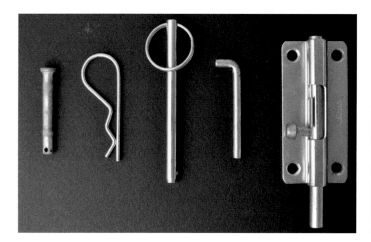

Figure 5-15: From left to right: clevis pin, R-clip, quick-release pin, hinge pin, and barrel bolt.

Figures 5-16 and 5-17: A solenoid pulls the pin of this kabuki drop mechanism when power is supplied.

As mentioned in the previous chapter, a **linear solenoid actuator** moves a steel plunger when energized. It can either pull it in or push it out. Some have springs to allow the plunger to return to its resting position when the electricity is turned off. The movement is sudden, instantaneous, and short.

Pull solenoids are perfect for pulling a pin in all the previously mentioned tricks. A push solenoid can be used as a hammer to knock something down or to break a breakaway prop.

When searching for solenoids, you may need to call it a "linear solenoid actuator" so you do not accidentally buy a solenoid valve, which we talk about in the next chapter.

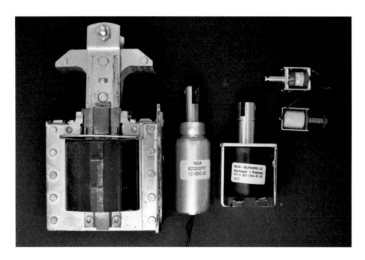

Figure 5-18: On the left is an AC-powered solenoid. In the middle are two DC solenoids with different housings. On the right are two miniature DC solenoids, useful for very light applications, like holding up a piece of paper. These are all pull solenoids except the yellow, which is a push solenoid; the pin extends out to the left, while the spring on the right retracts it when the power is turned off. The plunger in the AC solenoid is captive and cannot be removed, but the plungers in all the DC solenoids here will fall out if extended too far.

A 12VDC solenoid can be pretty tiny, and does not have much strength. The plunger needs to be able to move in a straight line or it will bind up and get stuck. If you have a pin holding up a lot of weight, a DC solenoid might not have the power to pull it free. You will need to design the trigger so it can be pulled with a minimum of effort, or switch to an AC-powered solenoid which is strong enough to pull a donut away from a stagehand.

Springs

A spring is a device which changes its shape when a force is applied, then returns to its original shape when the force is removed. While it is deformed, it stores a lot of energy; this energy is released as the spring returns to its resting state. For prop effects, the spring is often held in its energized position. The spring is released when the effect is triggered, powering whatever motion the prop needs. It is the same idea as gravity tricks, except the spring can move with more speed then gravity and in any direction.

Coil springs are the archetypal spring made of a coil of metal. They mainly come in two varieties: compression and extension. A **compression spring** gets squished as you push a force on it, and bounces back when released. An **extension spring** (also called a tension spring) is stretched as you pull on it with force.

A **torsion spring** works by twisting the spring. The spring on a mousetrap is a torsion spring. You can actually use a mousetrap as a trigger for your prop effect. Torsion springs are also used in spring hinges, another good mechanism to use in effects.

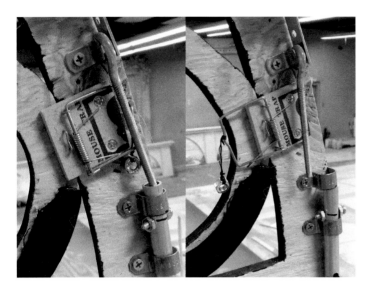

Other materials have spring-like qualities and can be used in place of metal springs. Elastic and rubber bands work well. Latex surgical tubing is like a heavy-duty rubber band with a lot more stretchiness.

Figure 5-19: A mouse trap is used in this effect to hit a piece of breakaway glass.

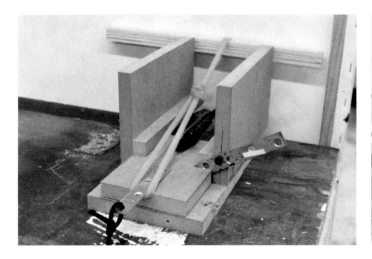

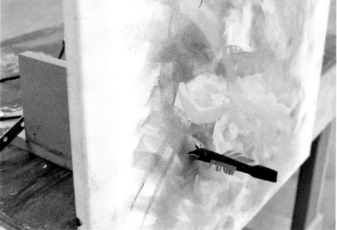

Figures 5-20 to 5-22: A loop of surgical tubing propels this crossbow bolt through a precut hole in the painting when released. The crossbow bolt moves fast enough that it appears to the audience that it was shot from the front. This is a common solution for when an actor needs to shoot a crossbow and throw a knife on stage; they pretend to throw the knife and then palm it while a double pops out of the painting or wall.

Electromagnets

An **electromagnet** becomes magnetic only when electricity is flowing to it. You can hold a piece of steel in place, and then drop it by turning the electricity off. For instance, an actor may need to stick a piece of paper to the wall, and then the paper needs to drop on cue at some later point. Attach a small bit of steel to the paper (perhaps disguised as a thumbtack which the actor pretends to press into the wall) and hide an electromagnet in the wall. The electromagnet can be controlled with a simple electrical switch.

You can also use electromagnets in conjunction with a magnetic reed switch. This allows you to have a portable prop set down on stage and then activated by the light board. The light board actually turns on the electromagnet which activates the reed switch inside the prop.

Drops

Some of the most magical moments in theatre come when snow begins to fall from above. Other light objects can rain down from the grid: flower petals, confetti, leaves, and pages from a book. While full-stage snow drops are typically the responsibility of scenery, props is often asked for smaller-scale drops, and the mechanisms are very similar.

For a sudden "dump" of material, you can use a fabric cradle with a kabuki drop mechanism. To avoid the material from clumping all together, it should be lightly fluffed and perhaps sprayed with static guard when it is loaded. With a few of these scattered around the grid, you can have a sudden burst of confetti over the whole stage for that climactic moment.

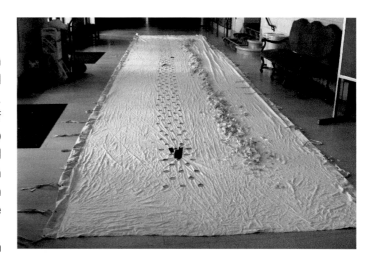

Figure 5-23: A full-stage petal drop. Each edge is hung from a separate batten so the whole cloth hangs in a "U" shape. San Francisco Opera. Photo courtesy of Lori Harrison.

For the gradual release of material over time, several methods are used. A traditional snow drop is a long cloth hung on two battens which can be flown in and out. A number of perpendicular slits or holes are cut along the center of the cloth. The cloth is filled with fake snow. To operate, first one batten is lifted and dropped, then the second batten is lifted and dropped.

Larger materials like leaves and petals may not easily fall from a traditional snow drop. One device that is useful acts like a conveyor belt, where a long length of fabric is unwrapped from one axle as it is wrapped onto another. The two axles are connected so that a manual crank or motor can turn both at the same time. Start with the fabric on one roll, and as you roll it to the other roll, you place the petals or leaves on the fabric so they get rolled up with the fabric. When it comes time for the drop, you turn the crank so the fabric goes back to the first roll. The petals fall off the fabric. You can have very sustained drops lasting for several minutes with this method.

Bicycle Cable

Bicycle cable is a flexible tube with a cable inside that is free to slide back and forth. You can salvage them off bicycles (they are used for the brakes) or buy it in spools to cut to length. When the ends of the flexible cable are secured in place, the cable can be slid despite any twists and turns between the ends. It's a much more compact solution when you cannot fit multiple pulleys for a trick line to take a serpentine path.

You can make your own with aircraft cable running through flexible bicycle conduit or fishing line through flexible PTFE (Teflon) tubing.

A variation of this idea is useful for making flowers and other plants wilt. The stem is made of a hollow tube, with a rod inserted to keep it straight. As the rod is removed, the stem wilts.

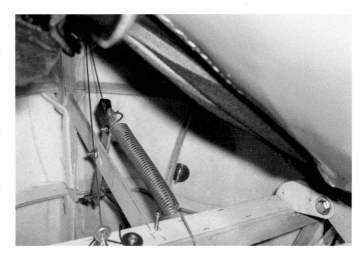

Figures 5-24 to 5-26: A bicycle brake handle is connected to a length of bicycle cable in this puppet jaw mechanism. When the handle is squeezed, it pulls the cable seen in the second photo, opening the jaw. When released, the spring pulls the cable back, closing the jaw. *The Magic Flute*, San Francisco Opera, 2012. Designed by Jun Kaneko. Photos courtesy of Lori Harrison.

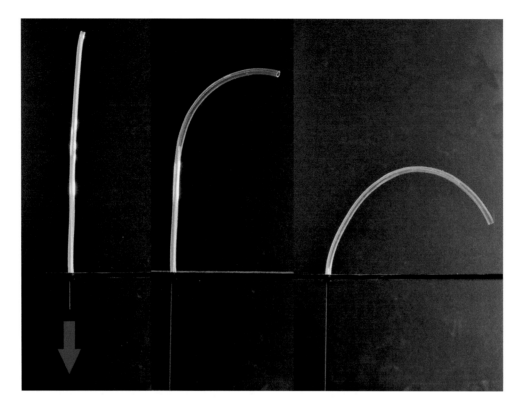

Figure 5-27: A wilting and reviving flower stem can be made from a green rubber or plastic tube. A stiff wire or rod is pushed up through the tube to straighten the stem, or pulled down to make it wilt. Attach leaves and flowers to the tube to complete the effect. This needs to be mounted to the ground with room underneath to operate it, or in a pot on a piece of furniture and operated from behind. Gang a few together to make a whole plant wilt.

six

pneumatics

Pneumatics use pressurized air to control props. It can be as simple as a burst of air that blows dust out of a book, or as complex as an animatronic figure controlled with multiple pneumatic cylinders. To build a pneumatic prop, you need to know how to obtain and contain pressurized air, how to transport it through pipes and tubes, how to control its flow with valves, and what mechanisms, devices, or tricks you can control with it.

Safety

First, some words about safety. Pneumatic systems can hold a lot of stored energy which becomes dangerous when released in an uncontrolled manner. Skipping or incorrectly doing even a single step can lead to injury. What follows is general advice; always be sure to follow the manufacturer's specific safety advice with any of their parts. Modifying the functional aspects of pneumatic parts can lead to unpredictable safety consequences.

- Point air cannons and outtake ports away from people at all times. The quick release of air can injure skin and eyes, or blow loose objects toward someone.
- Never add air to a prop until everything is secure. Be sure all tubing and fittings are securely connected, and that the prop itself is secured to the floor or wall. If handheld, be sure it is held firmly before filling it with air.
- Keep the air disconnected or emptied when the prop is not in use to avoid accidental firings.
- Only operate the electrical components at the correct voltage. Keep liquid and water away from electrical components.

- Use proper water traps in your airline and apply pneumatic oil to any parts that require it.
- Start with the air pressure as low as possible. Slowly increase the pressure until the prop functions the way it needs to.
- Use the least amount of PSI you can get away with. Most rods can operate successfully at less than 40 PSI (275 kPa). Never go above 120 PSI (825 kPa).
- Be sure to check the maximum PSI allowed for *all* of your components.
- Check that all your connections are secure.

What is Air Pressure?

Pneumatic props work when you have an area with higher air pressure meeting an area with lower air pressure. The air will move from the higher to the lower until the pressure becomes equal.

The pound per square inch, or PSI, is one of the main units we use to measure air pressure. It describes

The US and other countries on the Imperial system use PSI (pounds per square inch). Metric countries use kilopascals (kPa). You might also see the use of the bar in Britain, which is metric but not SI, and its use is deprecated. One bar equals 100 kPa.

1 PSI = 6.89 kPa	1 kPa = 0.15 PSI
20 PSI = 137.89 kPa	140 kPa = 20.31 PSI
40 PSI = 275.79 kPa	280 kPa = 40.61 PSI
120 PSI = 827.37 kPa	825 kPa = 119.66 PSI

how many pounds of force are being pushed against an area of one square inch.

At sea level, the pressure of the air around us is about 14.7 PSI (101.325 kPa). Most of the measurements used in this book and on the components you buy use **gauge pressure**, which is relative to the current atmospheric pressure. You pretend it doesn't exist; a tank with 1 PSI has a higher pressure than the outside air. On rare occasions, you may find the air pressure compared to a vacuum, known as **absolute pressure**. This is roughly equal to the gauge pressure plus 14.7.

The SI unit for pressure is kilopascals (kPa). One pascal is equal to one newton per square meter. Again, most of the components and gauges we use will measure kPa relative to the atmosphere.

For comparison, a sports ball holds about 12.5 PSI (86 kPa), automobile tires hold around 30 PSI (206.8 kPa), and the pneumatic tools in your shop run on 90 PSI (620.5 kPa). The human lung can generate 1 to 2.5 PSI (6.9 to 17 kPa). Do not underestimate what your lungs can do. It may seem silly, but sometimes the most complex tricks in theatre can be solved by having an actor sneak a small hose into their mouth and blow a quick puff. It removes so much complexity from the effect.

Props can get pressurized air from an air compressor, a tank of compressed air, or a hand pump.

Ideal Gas Law

The pressure, volume, and temperature of a gas is related to each other, and if you change one, the others will change as well.

$$\frac{P_1 \times V_1}{T_1} = \frac{P_2 \times V_2}{T_2}$$

In this equation, P needs to be the absolute pressure in PSI, V is the volume in cubic inches (in^3), and T is the absolute temperature in degrees Rankine (which is the temperature in Fahrenheit plus 459.67).

When you let pressurized air out of a tank, it will take up a lot more volume while decreasing in pressure. This makes the temperature drop. You notice this in high-pressure tanks, like CO_2 cartridges, which can freeze if the air escapes too quickly.

Air Compressors

Most shops already have an air compressor to provide power to pneumatic tools. A large stationary compressor may be used to power the entire shop, or small portable air compressors will be moved wherever needed. These portable air compressors can be set up backstage to provide air for a prop. If your shop is close to the theatre, you may even run a line from your large stationary compressor all the way to the stage.

Compressors are very loud when they are operating, and can be quite heavy. The air provided by them comes out in short bursts, which can create choppy motion in pneumatic parts. Most have a built-in air tank, known as an **accumulator**. This helps build up a reservoir of air and smooths the flow as it is used.

A compressor with a large-enough accumulator can be filled before the performance and then powered off; the stored air pressure will quietly power your pneumatic props.

Figure 6-1: Nearly every compressor you will find has a built-in accumulator. Only very small compressors, like those used for airbrushing, will not have an accumulator attached.

Long lengths of hose can lose pressure. If your compressor is far from the actual prop, a separate accumulator can be attached closer. It will help rebuild the pressure and act as a sort of "buffer" to provide full power to your props.

Air Tanks

For truly portable props, you can use just an air tank without a compressor. It is filled before the show with a compressor or hand pump, and then disconnected. You can also buy pre-filled tanks of air.

CO_2 cartridges are small tanks filled with compressed carbon dioxide used for paintball guns, emergency bike tire inflators, and more. A whipped-cream charger (a whippit or whippet) is a small canister of compressed nitrous oxide (N_2O) for making whipped cream. These are pressurized much higher than you will

ever need (often as high as 600 PSI or 4137 kPa). The one-time-use cartridges can be expensive to use for a long run. However, if you get the ones with threaded ends, you can fill them with 100 to 125 PSI (689 to 862 kPa) of regular air and have a very tiny reusable tank.

Paintball suppliers sell larger tanks of CO_2 as well. They also sell regulators and fittings for these tanks, making them easy to connect to a variety of other components. Again, these can be refilled with regular shop air.

I have never seen anyone using large gas cylinders (like those used for welding) or SCUBA tanks for props. They weigh a lot more than regular shop air tanks.

Metal water bottles should be avoided because you do not know what pressure they are rated to. Aluminum water bottles may burst, while steel flasks will usually pop their seal when filled with pressurized air.

Building Air Tanks

You can build your own air tanks using any rigid pipe meant for liquid and compressed air systems. Many of these materials, as well as some hoses, valves, and other components, can be found in the plumbing section of your hardware store.

Pipe and **tube** are two different things. Though both are hollow cylinders, pipe is built to carry fluids or gasses, so is engineered to withstand pressures from inside, while tube is built to be structural, so is engineered to withstand forces from outside. Use only rated pipes for compressed air; a random brass tube is not going to be the same as rated brass pipe.

Copper is great for compressed air. It is easy to work with, but expensive. It can come in very small diameters to save space with tiny effects. Joints can be

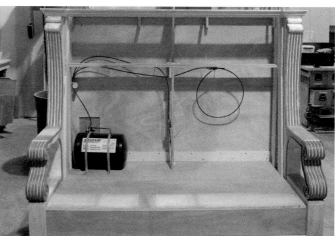

Figures 6-2 and 6-3: Air tanks come in a wide range of sizes. On the left is a 4 in³ volume chamber (65mL); on the right is a 5-gallon air tank (18L). Smaller ones exist, but are hard to find, while larger ones are too heavy for most props.

soldered or used with compression fittings. In the US, copper tubing is usually sold in one of three thicknesses: K, L, and M. The thickest is K. L is the most common (if you order and the type is not specified, it's usually L). M is the thinnest and not really safe to use with pressurized systems. It is usually reserved for draining unpressurized liquids. **Brass** is an alloy of copper, and they can be soldered together. Brass pipe itself is much more expensive than copper, but most fittings you find are made of brass.

Black pipe (steel pipe) is heavy and bulky, but is very cheap. Many theatres already have a stock of schedule 40 pipe on hand. **Stainless steel** is also good for compressed air, but prop builders rarely use it because of its weight and high cost. Galvanized pipe is not recommended for pneumatics.

The ends of both copper and steel pipe can be threaded and capped with fittings that adapt to a push-to-connect or quick disconnect fitting for easy hook-up to your prop. Copper can also be soldered to fittings and end caps.

PVC is not recommended for use with compressed air. It becomes brittle with age, and can shatter under pressure. When metal pipe and other plastic tubes fail, they tear or crack; when PVC fails, it explodes, with the resulting shrapnel causing lacerations and broken bones. PVC should only be used to carry liquids, as covered in the next chapter.

However, **ABS** pipe can be used for air. Properly glued joints are essential. The joints must be properly prepared, the correct adhesive applied, and the recommended curing time followed. Failure to do this can cause the joint to explode, which can also cause broken bones and torn skin (I've seen it happen).

I will reiterate that your props should use the least amount of pressure possible; if you find you need a lot more than 125 PSI (861 kPa), you probably need to redesign your trick. Design the gag so the pneumatic portion is triggering something else (like releasing a spring or pulling a pin). This will alleviate the need for potentially dangerous high pressure. Any rated metal pipe should handle 100 PSI (689 kPa) and below with no trouble.

Airflow

Besides the pressure, you also need to make sure your pneumatic system can move the correct volume of air fast enough to make your prop do what it needs to do. Your components will specify one of two methods for describing their rate of airflow: SCFM or C_v.

Standard cubic feet per minute (SCFM) measures how many cubic feet of air flow past a point within a minute. The "standard" part of the acronym sets the conditions to measure the flow at. It uses a pressure of 14.7 PSI absolute. Europe uses a standard temperature of 0°C (32°F), while the US may use 60°F (15.5°C), 68°F (20°C), or 70°F (21.1°C), among others.

C_v is the **flow coefficient**, or coefficient of velocity. It allows you to compare the flow through different valves, tubing, and other parts.

Your pneumatic cylinder will require a certain C_v to operate at the speed you want. Larger cylinders and faster speeds require a higher C_v. Any tubing, valves, or fittings between the cylinder and your air supply with a lower C_v will limit the flow down the line. In other words, the flow of your whole system is determined by the component with the weakest flow.

Troubleshooting

First, check the whole system for leaks and kinks. Leaks happen frequently at fittings which have not been properly tightened or sealed with Teflon tape. Cheap components may be inherently leaky because of ill-fitting gaskets. Your tubing may have gotten a hole in it somewhere. Be sure all your tubing is free of kinks, too.

Air pressure is lost over the length of tubing, so design your system to use the shortest amount of tubing possible. Even a straight line of tubing reduces air speed. For a self-contained pneumatic prop, this loss is negligible; we can usually just assume a 5 to 10 PSI drop (34 to 69 kPa) for all tubing and fittings combined. However, if you are running a 300' hose from your shop compressor to the theatre to power your prop, you may find a much bigger drop.

For pipes ½" in diameter and smaller, assume a 10 percent drop in pressure for every 100' (30m) of pipe. Larger diameter pipes will have about a 5 percent drop in pressure per 100'.

Every fitting will cause the air pressure to drop too, so use the most direct connections you can, rather than stringing together a chain of adapters.

Recheck your calculations. Remember that pressure is lost in every component of your system. If your cylinder requires a C_v of 0.63 to operate at your desired speed, a valve with a C_v of 0.63 may be too weak if it is followed by a push-to-connect fitting and several feet of thin tubing.

Remember that the flow of your whole system is determined by the component with the weakest flow. Your cylinder may fire with the perfect force and speed when hooked directly up to your compressor, but when you introduce all the tubing, valves, and fittings, you may find its performance lacking.

You can add a small air tank immediately before your valve and cylinder if you are still having sluggish parts. This **accumulator** is fed from the main supply, and lets you build up a large volume of air that only has to run through a short length of tubing with minimal fittings.

Airline and Hose

Props almost exclusively use flexible hose, or **airline**, to carry air. Unlike rigid pipe, you do not have to be so precise with your positioning, you can run hose around slight curves and corners without needing additional fittings, and you can quickly move, add, or replace parts as you prototype your trick.

The pressure ratings vary a great deal because wall thicknesses are not standard. A lot depends on the actual wall thickness, and the specific chemical content of the plastic. Always check the specific tubing you are buying. Some will list operating or working pressure while others will list the maximum pressure. You may also find the "burst pressure," which is exactly what it sounds like. Not all flexible tubing is necessarily made for pneumatic purposes.

Polyurethane is the preferred material for pneumatic applications. It has a good mix of flexibility and strength, and easily fits into many pneumatic push-to-connect fittings.

Vinyl (PVC) tubing can also be used. Some clear vinyl tubing is FDA-approved for food and beverage use (which will come in handy in the next chapter).

Nylon is stronger than polyurethane but far less flexible. **Natural rubber** (latex) is typically avoided in shops because of potential allergic reactions.

Any of the hose materials mentioned above can also come in braided versions, which add significant strength.

Airline tube is measured by OD. Common sizes for pneumatics include:

US	Metric
$1/8$"	3mm
$5/32$"	4mm
$3/16$"	5mm
$1/4$"	6mm
$5/16$"	8mm
$3/8$"	10mm
$1/2$"	12mm

The sizes in each row of this chart are comparable but not interchangeable. A 6mm tube in a ¼" fitting will leak.

Threaded Fittings

Many pneumatic components have threaded ports. If rigid pipe has a threaded end that matches, it can be screwed right in. For flexible tubing, you will need to attach a push-to-connect fitting or a hose barb to the threaded port.

Props people encounter six major types of threads. The thread standards may be US, British, or metric. Within each of these standards, the threads are either tapered or parallel (straight). Tapered threads form a seal when attached together to allow the leak-free transport of liquid or air.

The chart on page 90 lists the characteristics of these six thread standards. If you find a part that says it has R1/4 ports, you know it is a British Standard Pipe Tapered thread with a ¼" nominal size.

UN threaded connectors use common bolt and machine screw terminology. The first number is the diameter, the second is the TPI (threads per inch), such

The **male** end is the shaft with threads around the outside, while the **female** end is the hole with the threads on the inside. If you have two of the same kind, you will need an adapter to connect them together.

When ordering parts, the thread size should be indicated with the item's specifications. If buying parts from a store, it should be indicated on the component or the packaging. If you find a part with no indication of what the thread is, you need to test it with another part that you do know. Be careful, some noncompatible threads are close, and may seem to fit for a turn or two, but if you force the part in, you will damage the threads.

as #10-32. If you have a #10-32 male thread, you can use regular #10-32 bolts and other hardware on it, or even drill and tap your own threaded holes.

National pipe thread (NPT) is a US standard for tapered threads on pipes and fittings. Common nominal sizes for smaller props are ⅛, ¼, ⅜, and ½. NPT fittings are not compatible with regular nuts and bolts. Male and female NPT threads may also be referred to as MNPT and FNPT (or even MPT and FPT). NPT is the same as Iron Pipe Size (IPS) and male and female connectors may be denoted as MIP and FIP respectively. A female ⅛" NPT connector is the same as ⅛ FPT and ⅛ FIP.

British Standard Pipe (BSP) is the standard outside of the US. These can be either straight threads (indicated by G, BSP, or BSPP), or tapered threads (indicated by Rc, BSPT, R, or PT). The Japanese Industrial Standard uses British Standard Pipe Thread, but denotes straight threads with PF and tapered threads with PT.

NPT and BSP are roughly comparable in size, but the fittings cannot be used interchangeably. They also use nominal sizes, which do not correspond with either the OD or ID. For instance, a ½" NPT pipe is closer to ¾" in diameter. Nominal sizes simply indicate compatibility; a ½" NPT pipe will fit into a ½" NPT fitting.

Metric straight thread connectors also use the same terminology as metric bolts. The diameter is specified in millimeters. Unlike bolts, they usually do not give the length. The pitch (distance between threads) is either coarse or fine; it is usually coarse, especially if no pitch is indicated. Tapered threads will add the word "keg" or "taper" after the size.

Thread type	Abbrev.	Taper	denotion	example	synonyms
Unified Thread Standard	UN	parallel	size-pitch	#10-32	SAE
National Pipe Thread	NPT	tapered	nominal size "NPT"	1/4 NPT	MPT/FPT, MIP/FIP
British Standard Pipe Parallel	BSP	parallel	"G" nominal size	G3/8	PF
British Standard Pipe Tapered	BSPT	tapered	"R" nominal size	R1/2	PT
Metric Parallel		parallel	"M" diameter	M8	
Metric Tapered		tapered	"M" diameter "keg/Taper"	M5 keg	

Connecting Threaded Fittings

Straight threads need a rubber O ring to help seal any gap. Most fittings will come with one already on the threads. Tapered threads may have self-sealing threads (you will see white stuff on the threads). Otherwise, you will need to apply pipe joint compound or pipe thread sealant tape (aka PTFE or Teflon tape).

Apply pipe joint compound with a brush, small piece of wood, or your hands (if wearing gloves). Brush it on both the threads of the one fitting and on the inside of the other before attaching them together. The compound will expand as it dries and fill the gaps in the threads.

With pipe thread sealant tape, use ¼" wide tape on $1/_8$ inch, ¼ inch, and $3/_8$ inch male tapered pipe threads. Use ½" wide tape on ½ inch and larger male tapered pipe threads. When you disconnect a fitting, you need to remove the old tape and reapply fresh tape.

Figure 6-4: Begin at the open end of the pipe. Wrap the tape under tension in the direction the thread turns. Each layer should overlap the previous one by a half to two-thirds. Wrap until the entire threaded portion of the pipe is covered. Do a minimum of three full turns.

Both tape and compound come in several varieties that are approved for specific applications. Generally, use pipe joint compound for permanent connections and sealant tape for temporary or removable connections.

If your connection is leaky, you need to disconnect it and try again. Do not try to plug a leak by wrapping tape or fabric around the outside. You may have under or over tightened the threads. The threads may also be damaged, or the parts may have been cheap to begin with. Double check that the threads actually match and are not just a close fit.

Push-to-Connect Fittings

With **push-to-connect** (PTC or "Push-Quick") fittings, an airline tube is connected simply by pushing it into the collet. They can be disconnected by pushing the collet down and pulling the airline out. They allow you to quickly assemble components and make easy adjustments.

The cheap ones may only have a pressure rating of about 150 PSI (1034 kPa), which is fine for most of your prop needs. You can find higher-end fittings that are rated for higher pressures (though your tubing may not be rated as high).

When buying these, specify what OD tubing you need to connect to the collet, and what kind of threads you need to attach to your component. Most will have a male end, though you can find female ends for those truly bizarre situations. Also available are couplings to attach two tubes together (either the same diameter or two different diameters).

The following charts indicate which diameters of tubing work best with various threads, as well as which combinations are either hard-to-find or nonexistent.

thread	Tubing Diameter					
	$1/8$"	$5/32$"	$1/4$"	$5/16$"	$3/8$"	$1/2$"
#10-32	X	o	o	–	–	–
$1/8$ NPT	o	o	X	o	o	–
$1/4$ NPT	o	o	o	X	o	o
$3/8$ NPT	–	o	o	o	X	o
$1/2$ NPT	–	–	o	o	o	X

thread	Tubing Diameter					
	3mm	4mm	6mm	8mm	10mm	12mm
M3	X	o	–	–	–	–
M5	o	X	o	–	–	–
M6	–	X	o	–	–	–
M7	–	o	X	–	–	–
BSP $1/8$	–	o	X	o	o	o
BSP $1/4$	–	o	o	X	o	o
BSP $3/8$	–	–	o	o	X	o
BSP $1/2$	–	–	o	o	o	X

X denotes the optimal thread and tubing combination
o denotes possible thread and tubing combinations
– is not recommended or not available

Figure 6-5: Though your components may have a variety of port sizes and threads, if you buy push-to-connect fittings for the same diameter tubing, they can all connect together quickly and easily. Just keep the PTC fittings connected, and you have a supply of interchangeable components ready to assemble.

Quick Release Connectors

A quick release connector is useful for props where you regularly need to connect and disconnect a larger hose, such as attaching it to your compressor to fill the tank before every show, or making a prop with modular mechanisms that can be reused for future props. Your shop probably has quick connect plugs on all their pneumatic tools, so they can easily be attached to air hoses with quick connect sleeves.

Most shops use the **Industrial** style for their tools. This is the most popular style of plug sold in big box stores, and it often comes pre-packaged with pneumatic woodworking and construction tools. Another popular type is the **Automotive** (or True-Flate) style of plug, which is used, surprisingly, in automotive shops. You can find **Universal** couplers which are compatible with both Industrial and Automotive fittings (as well as a third style of fitting known as ARO).

Figure 6-6: The plug and socket of a quick release connector.

The different styles of quick connectors are not interchangeable, so be sure to buy the correct one. It is helpful to pick one style of quick connect and stick with it for all of eternity, so that no matter what part you grab in your shop, you know it will be the right kind: they all look very similar to each other.

The socket should be on the part leading to the air source, while the plug is connected to the part leading to the output. You want a socket with a built-in shut-off, so the air does not leak when it is disconnected. Most plugs remain open so the mechanism is depressurized when it is disconnected, but you can also find plugs with a built-in shut-off if you need the air to remain in the system after disconnect. Be careful when disconnecting a quick connect: a lot of air can be stored in the system, and it all comes rushing out as you disconnect it. The hose will whip violently away from you if you are not holding both ends.

Hose Barbs

A barbed hose fitting is pushed inside a tube to connect it. Barbed fittings restrict the flow of air since they go inside the tube, as opposed to push fittings which attach on the outside. Some sizes can cut the rate of airflow in half. However, brass barbed hose fittings can withstand pressures up to 300 PSI, and they are much easier to find.

Hose barbs often require one or two hose clamps tightened on the outside to prevent leaks.

Valves for Controlling the Flow

A **regulator** adjusts the air flow (PSI) coming through an airline. If you fill an air tank up to 100 PSI, the pressure will drop as soon as you begin emptying the air tank. To keep the pressure in your system at a constant 100 PSI, you need to fill the air tank up *greater* than 100 PSI, and put a pressure regulator on it that will drop the pressure to 100 PSI in the hose coming out.

A **check valve** only allows air flow in one direction. These can especially be helpful, as shown in the next chapter, when you have air and liquid mixed, so you do not have the liquid flowing back into the pneumatic parts.

A **Schrader valve** is the type of valve found on the outside of tires. They are sometimes called "tire valves," though other styles of tire valves exist. A tire valve is a one-way valve; it allows you to fill an air tank while preventing air from escaping.

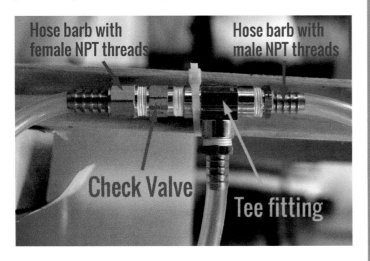

Figure 6-7: Various pneumatic parts.

Making a Champagne Cork Pop

Use a plastic champagne stopper with a hollow inside stem and a tubeless tire valve. Drill a hole through the cork that is just slightly smaller than the valve. Remove the metal nut and washer from the valve and push it up through the bottom of the cork until the rubber washer is seated against the bottom of the hole you drilled. Replace the washer and nut on top and tighten as much as possible.

Figure 6-8: Schrader valves on champagne corks. Photo courtesy of Patrick Drone.

Champagne bottles are designed to hold pressurized air; do not attempt this trick on wine or other bottles. Fill the bottle with liquid, attach the cork, and pressurize with 10 to 20 PSI (69 to 137 kPa) of air; this will vary depending on the effect you want, the amount of liquid inside, and other factors. If you use carbonated liquid, add less pressure, as the pressure will build up over time due to the carbonation.

Cover the cork with gold wrap foil and use a champagne cork cage to prevent the cork from popping prematurely.

A **ball valve** allows you to manually shut off air. You can turn a system completely off when working on it, or fill a tank from a source which is then disconnected. Ball valves also give you manual control over effects if you do not have the time or budget to add solenoids and electronics.

A **flow control valve** has a knob on top to adjust the speed through the valve. We usually put these on a pneumatic cylinder to control its speed. You can place the flow control valve on the input to control the speed when the cylinder is extending or on the exhaust to control it when retracting.

A **quick exhaust valve** allows air to be rapidly depressurized. It has three ports: air in, air out, and quick exhaust. When the air is exhausted, it leaves through the quick exhaust rather than back through the air line to the solenoid.

A **muffler** reduces the noise of the air being vented. A **breather vent** is a low-profile vent designed to keep debris from coming back into the airline or port. It also helps reduce the noise. A **pneumatic silencer** eliminates nearly all the noise from air escaping.

A **speed control muffler** attaches to the exhaust port and controls the speed of the air being exhausted while also muffling the noise. Like a flow control valve, it has one screw that controls the speed, and a nut to lock the screw in place.

Figure 6-9: A ball valve.

Air Cannons

An **air cannon** is a metal pipe that is open on one end and connected to a pressurized air source on the other. Small pieces of lightweight material are loaded in the open end. On cue, the pressurized air is triggered and it blows all the material out of the open end. Depending on the pressure, it can launch it quite high and far.

The material launched can be flame-proofed foam beads, ground-up cork, or the eponymous confetti used in a confetti cannon. Whatever is used should be lightweight enough that no one will be harmed should a stray piece hit them.

Great care must be taken that the pipe is not packed so tightly that the air has nowhere to go. The pipe should be able to withstand the air pressure being used: do not use a cardboard tube. As with other pneumatic tricks, you should not be using much more than 100 PSI. Do not be tempted to turn up the pressure to create a bigger "boom." Instead, try using lighter or smaller material, or reposition your tube. Alternatively, you can buy or rent professional air and confetti cannons that are engineered to deliver airborne material safely at higher pressures.

Pneumatic Cylinders

A **pneumatic cylinder** is designed to move and lift weight. A mechanical and electrical solution can require motors, gears, belts and chains to accomplish the same trick. A pneumatic cylinder simplifies these mechanisms. Some cylinders can hold a few ounces, others can handle several hundred pounds. If there are no leaks in the system, they can hold the weight indefinitely without burning up or wearing out. By controlling the rate of flow both into and out of the cylinder, you can control the speed at which it extends and retracts.

A **single-acting cylinder** (SAC) has one port. When air enters, it pushes the rod out. When the air is turned off, the rod is free to retract. Many single-acting cylinders have a spring to pull the rod back in; otherwise, the cylinder will only retract from the weight of the mechanism or if you manually push it back in.

A **double-acting cylinder** (DAC) has two ports for air. One pushes the rod out, the other pushes it in. The air exhausts out those same ports.

Other properties of a cylinder include the bore, stroke, and mounting option. The **bore**, or diameter, determines how much force the cylinder has. The **stroke** is the length that the arm extends. Mounting options vary greatly and depend on how you are using your cylinder. Some mounting options allow the cylinder to freely swing from the end, others bolt it squarely to your mechanism.

Speed of Pneumatic Cylinders Controlled by Valves

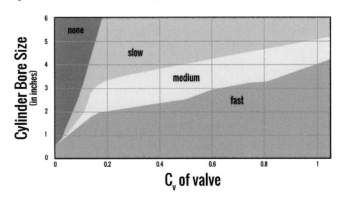

Figure 6-10: The flow of air allowed by your valve will determine the speed your cylinder moves at. You can calculate it out, or do a rough estimate based on the chart in this figure.

Your mechanism needs to be designed so the cylinder rod only moves in and out. It should not have to take any weight or forces to the side.

You cannot precisely calculate the exact speed of a pneumatic cylinder. Remember that the airflow to the cylinder itself depends on all the other valves, fittings, and tubes that come before it. Figure 6-10 gives a general indication of the C_v values your components need to make cylinders of various sizes move at certain speeds.

The more weight your cylinder has to push, the slower it will move. Make sure your cylinder is large enough to give you the maximum speed you might potentially want; you can always reduce the speed with flow control valves.

Solenoid Valves

A **solenoid valve** is a valve controlled by electricity. In a "normally closed" valve, the air flow stops when the valve is off. When the valve is powered with electricity, air can flow through it. Most valves you find are normally closed; you can find "normally open" valves as well, but we do not use those much in props.

The pressurized air source is connected to the "P" port on the valve. Your prop is connected to the "A" port. Air cannot flow from the A port back to P.

A valve with two ports like this is known as a 2-way valve. It is good for when you need a puff of air on cue.

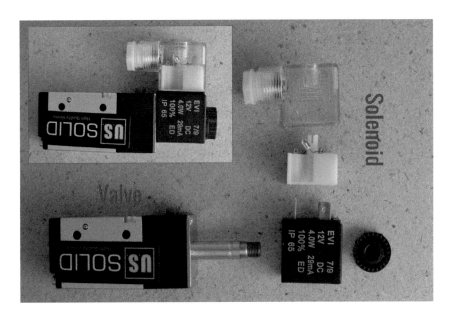

Figure 6-11: Most solenoid valves appear similar to this. You can usually separate the solenoid from the valve. Many come with a plastic enclosure around the wire hookups to protect from moisture when the valve is used for liquids. You can leave it off if you are using it for pneumatics. Only two of the terminals are used, while the third should remain unconnected. A solenoid valve is non-polarized, so you can attach the positive wire to either terminal and the negative to the other.

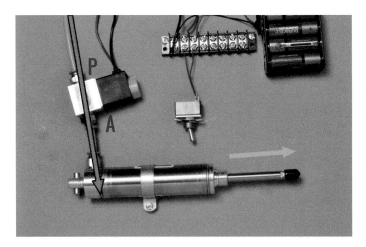 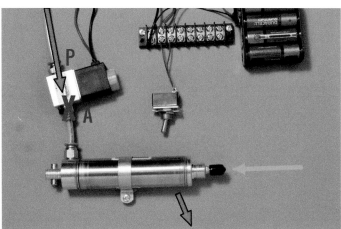

Figures 6-12 and 6-13: In a 2-way solenoid valve, air is free to move through the valve when the power is turned on. Air cannot travel through when the power is off. The air should only move in one direction, and the port where you hook up the pressurized air should be labelled "P." The other port is labelled "A." With a single-acting cylinder, the piston will extend when the valve is actuated. When the valve is released, air will slowly exit the cylinder through a tiny relief hole, and if the cylinder has a spring inside, it will return to its retracted position.

If you hook up a balloon to the A port, it will inflate when you turn the valve on. When you turn the valve off, it will remain inflated. What if you wanted the balloon to deflate when you turned the valve off?

A 3-way valve has a third port which is the exhaust for port A, or EA. When the valve is turned on, air flows from P into A. When the valve is turned off, any air that filled the components in A is exhausted through EA. A 3-way valve is used in a closed pneumatic system, when you need to fill a component with air on cue, but then empty it when the valve is switched off.

A 4-way valve adds a "B" port. When the valve is switched on, air from P flows into A, while any air in B exhausts out. When the valve is switched off, air from P flows into B, while the air from A exhausts out. So, if you have one balloon hooked up to A and one to B, A will inflate while B deflates, and vice versa.

In a 4-way 4-port valve, both A and B exhaust out of the same port. In a 4-way 5-port valve, A and B have their own exhaust ports (labeled EA and EB). If you want your cylinder to extend and retract at different speeds, you will need a 5-port valve so you can attach separate flow control valves to EA

For very small solenoids in tiny props, look for miniature solenoids such as the Clippard mouse valves, or those used in labs and medical fields. **Pinch valves** use the same principle, but simply squeeze the tube so nothing can flow past.

To sum up, a single-acting cylinder needs a 3-way solenoid valve and a double-acting cylinder needs a 4-way valve to both extend and retract on cue. If an SAC uses a 2-way valve, then the rod will need to be manually retracted, either through gravity, a spring, or pushing it by hand. The same is true of a DAC with a 3-way valve.

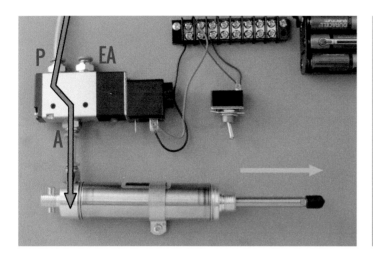 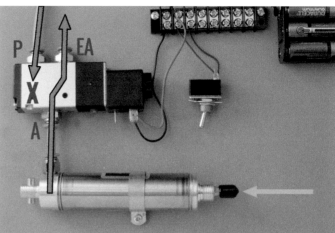

Figures 6-14 and 6-15: A 3-way valve has a third port labeled "EA" (for "exhaust A"). When the valve is turned off, any air that remains on the "A" side of the valve is exhausted out of EA. For a single-acting cylinder, this allows it to retract much faster. You can also add control valves to EA to slow down the retraction if needed. If you have a balloon or bladder hooked up to the valve, a 3-way valve allows it to be emptied.

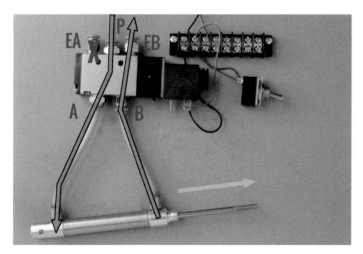 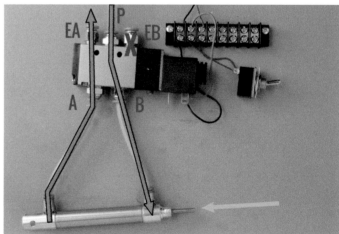

Figures 6-16 and 6-17: A 4-way valve is needed for a double-acting cylinder. When the valve is on, air flows into A and exhausts from B, filling the back of the cylinder and emptying the front, which extends the piston. When the valve is off, air flows into B and exhausts from A, which retracts the piston.

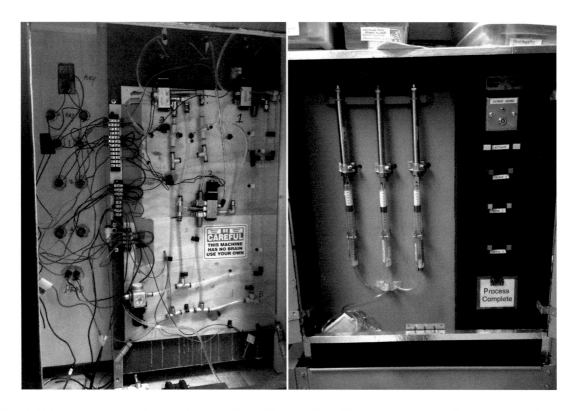

Figure 6-18: This lethal injection machine uses three double-acting cylinders. The grey valves with orange connectors are flow controls placed on the exhaust side of the valves, which help control the speed of the cylinders. *Dead Man Walking*, University of Michigan, 2014. Scenic design by Gary Decker. Photos courtesy of Patrick Drone.

seven

liquid delivery

Props need to control liquids for a variety of reasons. Many of our realistic kitchen plays require a sink with running water. Blood needs to drip, ooze, or spray from an actor or a prop. Vomit and urine are other bodily fluids that sometimes need to appear. While each of these have their own tried and true methods, any of them can be mixed and matched for more unique effects.

Pipe and Hose

The previous chapter compared various materials used to make pipes and hose. Many of the same materials used in pneumatics can also be used for liquids.

PVC is safe and highly recommended for conveying liquid, although not air. Copper can also be used, but PVC will always be cheaper and easier to work with.

For flexible tubing, garden hoses can be used, as can any of the flexible tubing mentioned in the previous chapter.

Drinking Water

If the actors will drink the water, you need to make sure every pipe and fitting is designed to be **potable**, or safe to drink. PVC pipe, copper, and flexible vinyl tubing are all usually safe for drinking water. Flexible polyurethane is usually not. The materials should indicate whether they are FDA-approved for transporting drinking water and beverages.

Used pipes and vintage faucets are a problem; if they have ever carried anything other than water, they may no longer be safe for carrying potable water. They can also be filled with rust or other buildup. Before giving anything to the actors, you should run water through the whole prop. The water should be colorless, free of particulates, and odorless. Buy a water purity test kit and use it on the water that comes out the other end.

Taste can also be an important factor for your actors. Many tubes and fittings made specifically for potable water are also designed to not impart any taste.

Any containers used to hold water during the show should be washed and refilled every day. You can also treat it with purification tablets (for treating drinking water while camping).

Connecting Hoses

Refer to the previous chapter on how to connect threaded fittings.

In the US and its territories, the thread standard for garden hose connectors is GHT ("Garden Hose Thread"). It is ¾" straight thread with a pitch of 11.5 TPI, and is used for ½", ⅝", and ¾" hoses. The BSP (British

Figure 7-1: A hose bibb valve (or bib) controls the release of water. The threads on the end allow a garden hose to be hooked up, or it can drain water right out into the open. It may also be called a bibcock, spigot, or tap.

Standard Pipe) standard, with a ¾″ straight thread and 14 TPI, is used outside the US. GHT and BSP are not compatible with each other.

Garden hose quick disconnects are useful to make your props modular, or for quick connection during a scene. *Saturday Night Live* famously uses garden hose quick disconnects for their vomit rigs.

Connecting PVC

PVC pipes and fittings can connect just by pushing them snugly together, but to avoid them popping apart from water pressure, you need to use PVC cement.

First, cut the end of the pipe squarely and cleanly. Round over the inside edge and bevel the outside edge. Scrub some **PVC primer** with a brush to the inside of the fitting and the outside of the pipe. Make sure it penetrates well and remains damp. Use a natural bristle brush to slather on a heavy coat of **solvent cement** to the pipe, followed by a thick coat to the inside walls of the fitting, making sure it does not run down into the fitting. While the surfaces are still wet, stick the pipe into the fitting all the way to the bottom. Use a strap wrench to help twist the pipe if you need help getting it all the way in. Let it rest undisturbed while it sets. Depending on the diameter of the pipe, it may be two to ten minutes before you can handle it. Wait one to four hours before you run water through it.

Running Water on Stage

The single most common running water effect on stage is a kitchen sink. We have a few basic ways for delivering running water which you can use or adapt. These methods are also useful for an onstage shower or a well pump. What you choose depends on the design and layout of your set, your theatre's resources, and the needs of the scene.

Hose from Backstage

If you have a sink backstage, you can simply connect a hose and run it to stage. The advantages of running a hose from backstage is that the water is clean and filtered (if using municipal water), you have an unlimited supply, and it is always under pressure.

The disadvantage is that you need a place to run and hide the hose, which is especially difficult when you have moving scenery. If the sink is emptied into a bucket, it can easily overflow if the water is kept on too long. Whenever possible, a second hose should be run to carry the water back to the building's drain. Finally, if a leak should ever develop anywhere along the line, it will continue to leak until the water is shut off, which could be disastrous if the leak develops overnight when no one is around to catch it.

Gravity Feed

For a gravity-fed system, a large container is placed a few feet higher than the sink. A 5-gallon (18L) bucket or water cooler bottle often does the trick, though a 55-gallon barrel may be needed for extended water-running scenes. It can be put on a platform or strapped to the back of a flat. Be sure to keep it covered so dust and debris from the stage does not get in.

The easiest way to run it is to siphon it. Run a hose or tubing from the bottom (clamped or fastened so it stays in place down there). Then when you bleed the lines, the water should flow through the hose whenever you turn on the faucet at the sink. You can also install a ball valve near your container to give you the option of shutting off the water before it hits the faucets. This is especially handy if you need to disconnect the water supply from the sink.

A long piece of pipe can store water and fit into shallow areas, like the space between two walls. A 6" PVC pipe that is 4'-0" long will hold 5 gallons of water. The bottom can be fitted with an adapter to connect the pipe to a hose, while the top can be capped with a threaded end cap, allowing you to open the pipe to refill it.

The advantages of gravity-fed systems are the simplicity and low cost. Any leaks will only spill as much water as the tank holds. The disadvantage is the weight; the more water you need, the heavier it gets. Water weighs 8.322 pounds per gallon ("a pint's a pound the world around!"), or 1kg per liter. That is 41 pounds for 5 gallons and 18kg for 18L. The wall behind the sink needs to be able to support that weight.

Garden Sprayer

A garden or "Hudson" sprayer moves liquid with air pressurized by a hand pump. Many brands exist, though Hudson is one of the better known, especially in theatre circles. Do not take one of the painter's Hudson sprayers

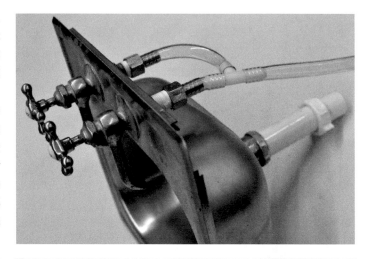

Figures 7-2, 7-3, and 7-4: A garden sprayer has a built-in hose. The end can be cut off and a hose barb inserted. A faucet typically has ½" NPT male threads on the bottom, though that can vary, especially with older faucets. All you need to do is find the right adapters to go from the hose barb to the thread.

to run water; use a new one, or one that has been set aside solely for water.

They come with a wand on the end of a hose; cut it off, then find a hose barb or push-to-connect fitting that fits the end of the open hose. Standard plumbing parts will get you the rest of the way to the sink. You simply fill the sprayer, close it, and pump it up until you have enough pressure.

This system is easy, inexpensive, and self-contained. Unlike gravity-fed systems, you can put the sprayer under the sink, which is great when your sink does not have a wall behind it or the wall cannot support the weight. You can often "dress" it so it looks like it is a bucket underneath the sink cabinet.

These tanks do not hold much water, though. Most will only hold 2 or 3 gallons, though some backpack sprayers can hold 5 gallons. The pressure also drops off as you use it.

Pre-Charged Pressure Tank

An accumulator tank, or pre-charged pressure tank, is used in residential water well systems. It is a two-part tank with a rubber diaphragm inside dividing the space between the air and the water.

The advantage is its capacity; they can range from 2 gallons to over 300 gallons. The air is always there, so you do not need to hook it up to a compressor or pressurize it before each show.

They are designed to always be filled with water, so storing between productions can be tricky since it is very likely mold will grow inside; they are not designed to open up for easy cleaning.

Electric Pump

An RV pump typically runs off 12V electricity. It has two ports to hook up hoses. Water gets sucked in through one hose and exits out the other. When it is hooked up to a sink faucet properly with no leaks in the system, it will only run when the faucet is opened.

The downside is that it makes quite a bit of noise while running. It should be screwed down securely with rubber washers to minimize vibration, and it can be placed inside the sink cabinet or behind the set to further eliminate noise. The amount of noise varies between models, so test a few out before committing to one.

The advantage is that with a battery, it is a self-contained system that can live on moving scenery. It will not run out of pressure like a garden sprayer, though it is still limited by the amount of water in your container.

Hooking up to a Sink

If you have a new faucet and you are building your water delivery system from scratch, it is easy to stick with parts you buy at the hardware store so they all fit together nicely. However, you may be using an antique sink with nonstandard connectors, or your water delivery may be cobbled together from found parts. It may take a series of adapters and connectors to get the two hooked up to each other. In these situations, the easiest solution is to take the end of your sink and the end of your water delivery system to the hardware store and say, "I need this to connect to this." If you cannot bring anything to the store, you may need to just buy a whole bunch of parts to try out and return the ones you do not use.

If space allows, set up your sink to accept a garden hose. Do the same with your water delivery system. If

Figures 7-5 to 7-8: The RV pump pulls water from a refillable container and pumps it up to the faucets. We used braided PVC hose with hose clamps at the connectors because the pump creates a lot more pressure than a gravity or hand pump system.

you do this with all your sinks in stock and all your water delivery systems, you make it easy to mix and match sinks and water supplies for future productions. You do not have to continually strip parts from one sink to make another sink work, or constantly hunt for new adapters.

Most sinks have one input for hot and one for cold. Rather than running two lines for hot and cold, just connect them together with a wye or tee joint before connecting to your water supply. This way, both faucets can be used, but the audience cannot tell that the temperature never changes.

Draining

If you are using a water delivery system with a limited amount of water, you can place a bucket under the sink to catch all the runoff. Be sure the bucket is large enough to hold all the water that is in your system; if your sink is fed from a 5-gallon tank, you need at least a 5-gallon bucket to catch it all.

Run a hose from the sink drain to the bottom of the bucket to avoid the noise of splashing water as the water drains from the sink. Use a flexible hose rather than a rigid pipe so you can remove the bucket to empty it.

Smaller buckets can fit directly under the sink. Larger buckets may need to be placed elsewhere on set, with hose or pipe transporting the water from the drain. The water needs to move downhill from the sink, otherwise it will never drain. A few uphill bits of pipe are fine, as long as the overall path leads downhill.

If there is a floor drain or slop sink backstage, you can have the hose empty there. This way, you do not have to empty a bucket every night or worry about it overflowing. This solution is especially good if you are supplying the sink with a hose from backstage.

Bleeding the Lines

Before you run water for the first time, the hoses and pipes are full of air. Depending on the length of hose between the water supply and faucet, it can be a few seconds between the time the actor turns on the faucet and water begins running. As part of the crew's preset, they must "bleed the lines," or turn on the faucet just until water begins to come out. Then, when the actor turns the water on during the show, it will flow right away.

Fake Blood

Now we switch gears from water to blood. The principles are similar though it is done on a much smaller scale. Fake blood can either be bought or made in your shop.

Commercial blood brands include Ben Nye, Reel Blood, Pigs Might Fly, Gravity and Momentum, and many more. Each brand can come in a variety of forms, from thin liquids to thick pastes. Using a commercially available blood gives you consistency and reliability, and can save a lot of labor time with grocery shopping, testing, and preparing your own blood.

Some companies make a two-part compound called "magic blood." One part is a clear powder, the other is a clear gel, and when they come in contact with each other, they produce a blood color. This is good for small wounds but not for dripping cuts; it is useful when you have nowhere to hide a blood apparatus.

Even when buying in bulk, commercial blood solutions may still be too pricey for some shows. Nothing beats the convenience of running down to the all-night grocery store and buying the ingredients to make new blood for the morning, rather than waiting several days for your commercial blood to be shipped.

The old tried-and-true recipe involves just taking corn syrup and adding red food coloring (and a drop or two of blue and green) until it is the color you want. This is edible, but it is sticky and will stain nearly anything.

To avoid staining, use powdered food coloring rather than liquid; it can be bought in bulk for extra savings. However, some props people find the colors to be less consistent than liquid food coloring. Powdered beetroot is also very fugitive (the color washes out). Besides its appearance and non-staining properties, it is helpful if the blood needs to be ingested by an actor who has sensitivities to artificial dyes.

To avoid stains for a nonedible blood, add liquid dish detergent. You can use a few tablespoons per 16oz bottle of corn syrup.

You can also forgo the corn syrup and just use the liquid soap as a base. Liquid laundry detergent often has the proper consistency, and if you use one with a deep blue color, you only need a bit of red coloring to get the right appearance. Be gentle when mixing, as you can easily create bubbles or foam. If the blood has the possibility of getting near an actor's mouth or eyes, switch to baby shampoo or baby soap.

A final base is water-based lubricant. Personal lubricant, like KY Jelly, can be used, but bovine and equine lubricant are available in larger quantities at a lower price. It can be thinned to any consistency you need with water and tinted with food coloring or tempera paint.

Washable tempera paint is super cheap and very easy to clean up. It is harder to get the consistency right, but for standing pools of blood, it can be a helpful option.

If you need to darken your blood and make it more "goopy," try chocolate syrup or peanut butter (as creamy as possible; don't use the organic stuff here). Peanut butter has the additional advantage of making the blood easier to clean off fabrics.

The color of the blood depends on what type of wound it is. Blood from veins or extremities like fingers and toes is low in oxygen and appears darker. Bright red and spurting means it is coming from an artery and is for those potentially fatal wounds.

The lighting affects the appearance of blood. Darker scenes may require a more vibrant color. Blood which soaks into darker fabrics may appear black. Sometimes you need to mix up a cartoonish shade of red just to make it appear correct under lights.

There is no universal blood recipe because each production has its own variables. I could spend the entire chapter giving different recipes, but this is not a fake blood recipe book. You can find lots of information online about how fake blood was made for various productions. If you see a show with amazing fake blood, you can contact the prop master and they will often be more than happy to share how they did it.

Blood Sponges and Bags

A **blood bag** is a thin plastic bag holding some liquid blood. It is hidden somewhere on the actor's costume, or somewhere on the set where it can be palmed before needed. When squeezed, it breaks and allows the blood to spill out. With a bit of air inside the bag, it can also "pop" with a small burst of blood flying out.

A plastic bag sealer (or impulse sealer) uses heat to fuse two sheets of plastic together. Fuse all four sides and you have a closed pouch. The plastic comes in rolls in a variety of thicknesses. You can also seal the open end of a plastic bag (like a sandwich bag). This lets you make a blood pouch to whatever size and proportion you need, filled with however much blood you need. A Seal-A-Meal vacuum sealer machine works the same way; often, you do not want to use the vacuum setting, because a little bit of air in the pouch makes it pop easier.

Thinner bags are easier to pop and burst by hand. Thin vegetable bags from the supermarket are great, though most of those have writing on them. If the action is rougher, or you need a very large pouch, you may need a thicker plastic to prevent your bag from breaking before the cue. In this case, an actor may need a "blood ring," which is a ring with a thumb tack soldered to the back. This allows them to pierce and slice open the bag.

A **blood sponge** is a sponge soaked in fake blood. Every time the actor squeezes it, a bit more blood comes out. You can use a small natural sponge, or cut up a regular kitchen sponge.

If you need a blood bag to burst on an actor as if from a gunshot, you can glue a washer to the outside and tie a string to the washer. When someone yanks the string, it will pull the washer and rip the bag open.

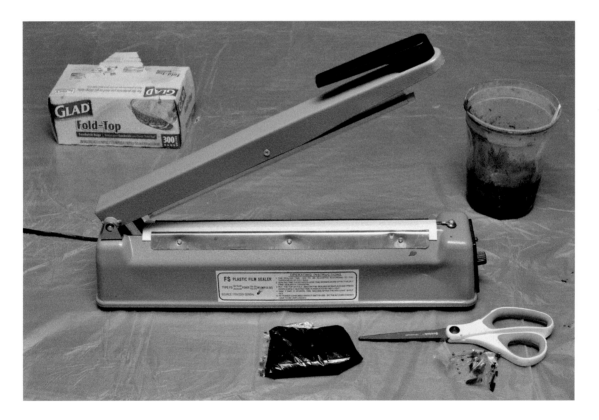

Figure 7-9: An impulse sealer is a helpful tool for making blood bags. The thin "fold-top" sandwich bags work well; the reclosable Zip-Loc bags are a bit thicker and more difficult to break. Fill the bag with the amount of blood you need, seal the top closed and cut away the excess. You can then rotate the bag and seal one of the sides to make it even smaller.

Figure 7-10: A blood sponge and a blood bag can be combined to give the effect of a sudden injury which continues to bleed as the actor holds the wound. One way to construct it is with plastic cling wrap and thread.

Figure 7-12: When squeezed, the bag will burst. The more you squeeze, the more blood will ooze out of the sponge.

Figure 7-11: The sponge is thoroughly soaked in blood and wrapped in the plastic. The end is tightly twisted shut. Leave a bit of air in your bag so it is easier to "pop." Wrap the thread around the end to keep it from winding back open.

Manual Blood Delivery

Blood and other bodily fluids can be dispensed from any number of items: syringes, bulb syringes (ear wax and baby snot removers), turkey basters, squirt bottles (for kitchen or bath), plastic pipettes, eye droppers, squeeze bulbs, squirt rings (a novelty gag item with a squeeze bottle attached to a ring), and bento box soy sauce containers. A little bit of blood can have a big impact.

With some of these containers, the surface tension of the blood is strong enough to keep it in until you squeeze; for others, they will leak unless you close them up somehow. If the container has a removable lid, you can stretch a bit of plastic wrap between the lid and the container. When you squeeze it, the plastic will pop and the blood will squirt out. If your container does not have a lid, cap the end with a bit of caulking putty (like Mortite)

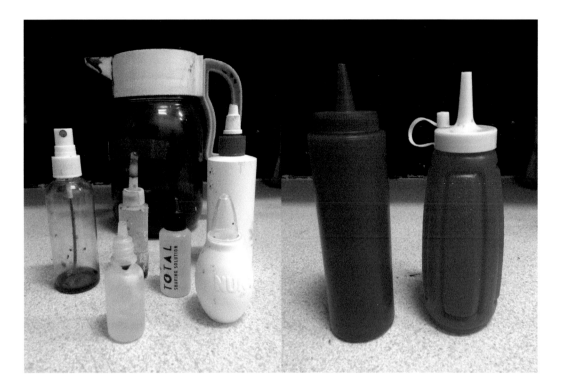

Figure 7-13: Some blood dispensers include travel-size spray bottles, various squeeze bottles, bulb syringes, and ketchup bottles. Photos courtesy of Eimer Murphy.

or oil clay to keep the blood from dripping out. It should become dislodged when the container is squeezed.

Surgical tubing or any of the tubing previously mentioned can be run from the container to have the blood emerge wherever you need it. The tubing can be sewn to the inside of the actor's costume or to an undergarment. The squeeze bottle can be concealed in a bulky part of the costume, like the pockets, or under a ruffle, while the tubing can run almost undetected to wherever the wound is inflicted.

The tubing should be **primed**, or filled with blood, before it goes out on stage. If you leave it full of air, it can take a few moments for blood to exit the end of the tubing after you squeeze your container. Priming it will make the blood come out instantly upon squeezing.

If the action of the scene allows it, you can sew a small "loop" in the tubing near the end. This acts like a plumbing trap, holding the blood inside but preventing it from exiting prematurely.

Bigger bags can be concealed in a special pocket sewn under the armpit. The actor can squeeze it just by pushing their arm against their side. A medical catheter bag has one-way valves to make them easy to fill and empty. Water bags for hiking are also useful, as they have a variety of fittings, caps, tubing, and valves to attach and customize your rig.

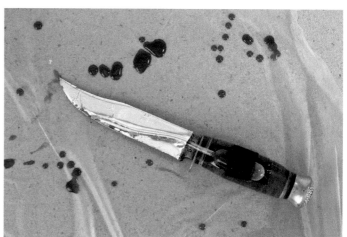

Figures 7-14 and 7-15: You can easily adapt any knife into a blood knife if it will only be seen from one side. Attach a pipette to the handle and run a small length of tubing to the edge of the knife blade. Some foil tape will hold the tube in place and match the appearance of the blade (you can paint the foil to further mimic the metal of the blade).

Figures 7-16 and 7-17: As the actor runs the blade over the skin, they squeeze the pipette to push the blood out. With a bit of practice for timing, it will look like the knife is cutting a wound which bleeds. The pipette will remain hidden by the actor's hand. Make the pipette removable so that you can refill it with blood for every performance.

Blood Knife

A blood knife is a specially prepared knife that administers blood as it "cuts" an actor. The simplest type of blood knife has a container of blood hidden in a hollow handle. The handle needs to be flexible enough to allow you to squeeze the container, or it can be open on one side. A thin tube runs from the container to the edge of the blade; when the container is squeezed, the blood will appear along the cutting edge of the blade. If the scene is staged so that you only see one side of the blade, the tubing can run along the upstage side where it is never seen. The most sophisticated blood knives have the tubing run inside of the knife blade, so it remains hidden no matter how close you are or what angle you view it at.

Keep it Simple

Hide a bowl of blood on set that an actor can dip her hands into and then wipe on the wound during a struggle. Use a towel to conceal some blood that the actor can wipe onto their sword or shirt. An actor may be able to sneak a "drink" of blood and then let it run out of their mouth later in the scene.

The simplest tricks are the easiest to keep consistent. A radio-controlled pneumatic effect has many parts that can break and many opportunities for failure. Complex effects should only be used when they can produce a moment that is noticeably better than a simple effect.

Figures 7-18 and 7-19: A ball valve with a flattened flared top was added to a hot water bottle for this vomit "gag." It was set into a foam square which was covered to look like a pillow. The actress could handle the pillow however she wanted. When it came time to throw up, she slipped her hand into the pillow and opened the valve; she then hugged the pillow to squeeze all the vomit mixture out of the hot water bottle. It gave her complete control over the timing of the effect. *God of Carnage*, Royal Manitoba Theatre Centre, 2012. Designed by Gillian Gallow. Props built by Larry Demedash, and Kari Hagness. Photos courtesy of Kari Hagness.

Blood Rehearsal

Before getting to tech, it helps to schedule a "blood rehearsal" using water. Map out where blood will appear and how it might get there. A fight sequence might start with just a small smear of blood applied by the actors during a scuffle, followed by blood from a blood knife, ending with breaking a capsule of blood in the actor's mouth.

Rehearsing with water will help show where the blood ends up, and whether it gets on costumes, furniture, or rugs. It may reveal some surprises; the actor may have blood on their hands, and when they exit, they go through the door, leaving blood on the door knob.

Now you need to figure out a way to clean it off before the next actor touches it.

Pneumatic Blood Delivery Systems

A pneumatic system can force blood or other liquids out of a tube. Basically, it's like a pipette with blood, but instead of your hand squeezing the end, you have pressurized air pushing the blood out.

The blood should be kept in a rigid container. A soft bag like a catheter bag will just inflate as it is filled with air.

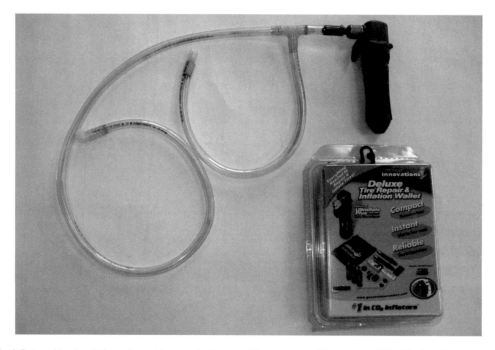

Figure 7-20: A bicycle tire inflator with a hand trigger is used to move the blood in this mechanism. The amount of blood in the tubes was enough for the effect, with no need for a separate container. The tubing splits into two so that blood can simultaneously come out the front and back of the actor. The whole mechanism was easily concealed in the costumes and triggered by the actor. *Tommy*, Dallas Theatre Center, 2008. Photo courtesy of Rick Gilles.

You do not want the liquid running back into the tubes carrying the air. You can use gravity to assist you: have the air run into the top of the blood tank, with the blood exiting out the bottom. A portable rig which does not always remain upright should use a check valve to allow the air into the tank while preventing the blood from flowing back.

With a properly designed system, 80 to 120 PSI (551 to 827 kPa) is all you need for a big splatter of blood against the wall. Use a pressure regulator to bring the pressure down to what the effect requires. You can bring it all the way down to 10 PSI (69 kPa) for an oozing trickle of blood.

A sample system will start with a pressurized air tank or be hooked up to an air compressor. Next will be a regulator or a flow control to deliver the exact amount of pressure you need for the effect. Follow that with an inline check valve to prevent the liquid from flowing back into the valve and tank. Finally, you will have your bottle filled with liquid. The lengths of tubing will vary depending on your needs; if it is meant to be hidden on an actor, you may want the bulk of the parts hidden in their pocket or somewhere else inconspicuous, while the bottle of liquid is closer to the exit point. The final length of tubing will carry the blood or vomit directly to the exit point.

Vomit Recipes

Recipes for fake vomit can vary greatly depending on what the director envisions for the scene. If your rig carries the vomit through tubing, you need to limit the amount of "chunks" and viscosity to keep the tubes from clogging. Brown and white food coloring often provide a good base; the white food coloring helps make the liquid opaque, otherwise it may look like juice or soda.

Another good option is thinned-down pea soup, especially instant pea soup. It does not need to be warm, but it should have been adequately cooked in the past so the vegetables are soft and do not clog the lines.

When you are dealing with liquids other than water, you may need to instruct the crew to flush the lines after every performance. Fake blood or vomit will dry to a crust inside the tubes that will impede the flow and eventually cause a clog.

Urination on Stage

The simplest method for an actor to relieve himself on stage is to palm a small water bottle and empty it upstage with his back to the audience. Any of the blood delivery methods can be adapted too. A small container of water can be hidden on the actor, with a tube running to his or her pants. A small hand-operated valve can control the flow right at the end of the tube.

If you need a more realistic way for your actor to urinate, you can find kits like the Whizzinator which are marketed as "novelty" fake urinating devices, but surreptitiously intended for passing a drug test under observation.

eight

breakaways

When a prop is broken on stage, the scene instantly gains more drama and excitement. However, if you do not properly plan how to do it, it can easily deplete your budget and steal all of your time.

We have two major categories of breakaways: a single prop which is reassembled after every show, or consumable props which are destroyed every show. For complicated objects, you can combine the two methods, and have part of the prop reusable and part of the prop consumable.

The first part of the chapter will discuss props that can be broken and reassembled, and the second part will discuss how to make single-use breakaways that are safe and cheap. We will also pay particular attention to breakaway glass, which poses its own unique challenges and appears in quite a few shows.

Breakaway Furniture

For wooden furniture and wooden objects, you can cut the prop apart where you want it to break and then hold it together with an easy-to-break and replaceable piece of wood. For a staff or rod, make a jagged cut so the break looks more natural. For chairs and stools, a natural breaking point is at the joints.

Drill holes into each side of the break and use a dowel or piece of balsa to reconnect them. The dowel or balsa breaks during the scene and is replaced after the show. A $^3/_{16}$" diameter dowel works well for chairs that need to be swung around. A $^1/_8$" dowel is easier to break, but is not as reliable if the chair is lifted and swung before breaking. The dowel can be scored slightly to make it easier to break. The pieces can be lightly hot-glued together for added sturdiness. Matchsticks and bamboo skewers can be substituted for the dowels,

Figure 8-1: Cut a staff apart so it looks like it is broken, and drill a hole through the center of each side the same diameter as a dowel. Score the dowel so it is easy to break.

Figure 8-2: The dowel will hold the two halves of the staff together. You may need a few dots of hot glue if you do not feel your connection is secure enough on its own.

Figure 8-3: After the actor breaks it, the remnants of dowel are removed from the holes and a new one can be inserted for the next performance.

and can give a rougher, more jagged appearance to the broken edges.

If a chair is breaking over another person, you may want to replace the seat with closed cell foam or replace the legs with rubber.

Breakaway objects will deteriorate over the run of a production, so build a few that can be swapped in as needed. For added durability, thread some lamp rod into the holes and insert your dowels into them. This gives you a metal edge to break the dowels against, which makes it easy to break and prevents the hole from widening over time.

Tie fishing line to the pieces to prevent them from flying too far away from each other. It will help with cleanup and reassembly after the scene.

Some chairs have the pieces assembled with hardware rather than glued joints. You can replace this hardware with Velcro to make an instant breakaway. It is also relatively easy to replace this hardware with magnets.

Magnets

Magnets are an ideal solution for many types of reusable breakaways. You want rare earth magnets, not craft or ceramic magnets. Shop online for the biggest selection in sizes and shapes. Especially useful are magnets with countersunk holes that allow you to screw or bolt them to an object. Be careful with polarity; the countersunk magnets can only face one way, and if you put them on opposite ends of a break, they will be positioned to repel each other rather than attract. You do not always need a magnet on both sides; you can have a magnet on one side and a thick piece of steel on the other.

Non-countersunk magnets can be adhered with epoxy adhesive. Often, the magnet is much stronger than the adhesive and will pull free. The best way to attach them is to make them **captive**, where they are physically encased in such a way that they cannot be pulled free. The magnetic force is still strong enough to

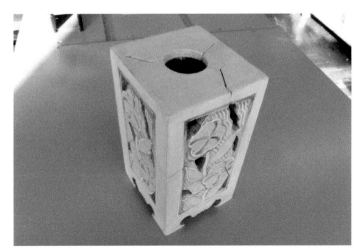
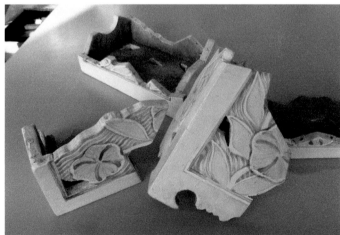

Figures 8-4 and 8-5: This wooden box was cut apart and magnets were hidden inside the edges to hold it together during the scene. *A Single Shard*, Seattle Children's Theatre, 2012. Designed by Carey Wong; built by Jake Nelson. Photos courtesy of Elizabeth Friedrich.

hold your prop together when the magnet is covered with a small layer of material.

You can put a lip around the hole where the magnet is to hold it captive. You can also drill a hole from the other direction without going all the way through and insert the magnet there. Use a Forstner bit to give your hole a flat bottom for the magnet to sit on. Alternatively, glue a fabric strip over the magnet, or sew the magnet between two layers of fabric.

Sitting on Breakaways

One of the trickier tasks is making a stool, chair, or bench that needs to be sat upon before it breaks. A seat that is sturdy enough to support a human body is usually too sturdy to be broken by an actor.

If possible, the chair should be switched out between being sat on and being broken. If that is impossible, you can have an extra chair on stage that no one sits on; with careful blocking, the audience will never notice that this chair is being avoided by the actors until it comes time to break things.

If it absolutely must be the same chair that is sat on and broken, you may need some kind of brace that spans one of the pre-broken seams and that can be surreptitiously removed by the actor right before the breaking occurs. Usually, a sliding bolt mechanism can be used or constructed. Look back at the chapter on trick mechanisms for ideas on using removable pins to hold a brace in place.

A Variety of Reusable Breakaways

As with furniture, many items can be broken ahead of time, and then held together temporarily. Cut the prop in pieces so the break lines are not too visible; if the piece has carved details or seams, these are good places to cut.

The piece can be assembled each night with a dot of CA glue (super glue), hot glue, double stick tape, rope caulk (Mortite), or wax; experiment to discover which adhesive works best on your material. Another way to hold the pieces together before the prop breaks is with "snot tape," also known as fugitive glue or credit card glue. Magnets are always great too. Depending on how close your audience is, you may even be able to get away with just using scotch tape across the seams.

Make a few duplicates for back-ups. If the crew accidentally breaks one during preset, they may not have time to reassemble it before the show begins. Again, pieces can be kept from scattering too far by attaching them together with fishing line.

What follows are a few common breakable items and examples of solutions.

For ceramic plates, melamine dishes can be pre-broken and then held together with scotch tape or dabs of hot glue. The pieces are nearly indestructible. When painted, they can look like a variety of ceramic plates from different periods. You can also find melamine plates with patterns printed on them that look indistinguishable from ceramic plates.

For a violin or other stringed instrument, the pre-broken pieces can be connected with a flexible fabric hinge. The strings can be lightly tacked in place with hot glue so they "snap" when the prop is broken.

Figures 8-6 and 8-7: This breakaway egg was made of foam and held together with magnets. The magnets were held in place with small Tyvek patches. *Rikki Tikki Tavi*, Seattle Children's Theatre, 2014. Designed by Jeff Cook; built by Daphne Maurides. Photos courtesy of Elizabeth Friedrich.

If a piece of fabric needs to be torn, it can be cut or torn beforehand and reattached with a few light stitches. Use small pieces of Velcro to hold it in place too.

The horn on a unicorn statue can be secured with a dab of hot glue each night. A typewriter can have a vacuum-formed shell with a slew of typewriter parts attached.

For a breakaway picture in a frame, the picture can be printed every night and perforated where you want it to tear. The frame can be balsa wood or pieces of wood held together with magnets.

If you can deal with seeing cracks ahead of time, you can cut plexiglass into jagged pieces and assemble them into a window pane. Hold the wooden frame together with magnets, or use a dab of hot glue to hold the plexiglass pieces together.

If your prop is made of a material which cannot be cut apart, you can make a mold and hollow cast it in resin.

A quarter of an inch (6mm) is sturdy but not too solid. This cast can be cut into pieces which are reassembled for every show.

Breaking Real Items

Depending on the piece, it may be within your budget to buy "real" items in bulk to smash every night. The items may need to be scored, which is a line cut partway through the material. This makes the item easier to break. It also helps you control where they break, making the breakage consistent from show to show.

For instance, it is often cheaper to find a bunch of vinyl records to smash than making a fake record. Score them with a knife to make a consistent breaking pattern.

One disadvantage is that many materials exhibit sharp edges when broken. They could break into many tiny shards which increase the cleanup time. This can be minimized by coating them.

Coating Props for Safer Breaking

The coating you choose depends on the material of your breakaway, the effect you are looking for, and what materials work with your budget and timeframe. Thicker coatings will prevent the pieces from separating at all, leaving an object which is crushed rather than obliterated. This deadens the sound a bit.

For glass, use a spray adhesive or PVA-based adhesive to **scrim** (closely cover) the outer surface with fine net. A flexible glue, such as book binder's glue, can help make the object "crunch" rather than shatter. Paint or spray some shellac or varnish over the top to make the fabric translucent again.

China, ceramics, and plaster can be scrimmed using butter muslin, cheesecloth, silk, or tissue paper. You can even paint over the top.

Some popular brands of coating materials include Jaxsan, Sculpt-or-Coat, Rosco Flexcoat and Flexbond, and Plasti-Dip. Each of these produce different results on different materials, so experiment to find the best results.

Uncoated areas are more likely to break. You can leave specific areas uncoated to encourage the prop to break along those areas. Scoring a line through those areas will make the breakage even more predictable.

A cheaper and quicker method is to wrap the prop in clear tape (particularly props with flat areas and simple curves). Try contact paper for flatter items like plates; it comes in clear or various colors and patterns. You can adhere it to the bottom to make it less noticeable.

For larger glass panes, you can use shatter-resistant security film for windows. This is especially

Figure 8-8: These mugs had a band of masking tape wrapped around in two places. The whole mug was then painted to hide the tape. This solution was the result of experimentation with these specific cups and the specific actor to make it break in a consistent and controllable manner. Photos courtesy of Nancy Wagner.

useful for mirror panes. Cover both sides with film or tape. You will get the effect of the spider-web crack pattern appearing without worrying about any pieces going anywhere. You can even put the mirror behind a piece of polycarbonate for maximum protection.

Balsa Wood

Balsa wood is easy to break and lightweight enough to smash over an actor without harming them. You can build entire pieces of furniture out of balsa wood, or just build the part that gets broken and color it to match the rest of the piece. Thin sheets can make all sorts of boxy props, like old radios. It may be too soft for some applications.

Balsa wood can be difficult to find in planks wider than 12" (305mm). If you need to make a breakaway desk top, you would have to join several planks together.

Food-Safe Breakaways

A plate which is eaten upon before breaking has the extra consideration of needing to be food-safe. You can seal the surface with a food-safe finish, but that can make it harder for the plate to break apart. Food-safe paraffin wax (the kind used in canning) is a good coating, since wax itself is used for breakaways. Heat the plate with a hot air gun before applying the wax. Shave the wax down; the plate should be hot enough that the shavings melt upon contact, and you can use a brush to spread the wax around evenly.

For a cup that you drink out of before breaking, you can seal the inside or insert a second, removable "cup" that holds the actual liquid. A false bottom gives the appearance of a full cup with only a small amount of liquid, thus minimizing the amount that gets on the stage when the cup is smashed.

Casting Multiple Breakaways

For the highest amount of dramatic impact, make a mold of a prop and cast it in a material which can be smashed to oblivion in every show. While this is costlier than a reusable item, and may not be as controllable, the sound and appearance of a material actually shattering is difficult to fake.

Plaster, wax, and clay are the most common materials used for opaque pieces. Transparent pieces require special attention and will be discussed afterwards.

Most of these props will be cast in two-part (or more) molds. Plaster and wax are cast best in silicone rubber molds. Clay should be cast in plaster molds. See my other book, *The Prop Building Guidebook*, for further information on making molds.

Plaster

Fill your mold with plaster and slush cast the sides, pouring out the excess. Let it dry thoroughly: wet plaster will be heavy and will not break as cleanly. It may take a few trials to find the thickness that works best. In some cases, it may be so thin you can almost see through it. The plaster can be sealed with shellac and painted.

A balloon can be used as a form for plaster vases and vessels. Fill the balloon and coat it with plaster. After the plaster dries, pop the balloon, and you are left with a hollow piece. Cover it halfway to make a bowl, and higher up to make more of an egg shape.

Add parts on the outside and loose guts on the inside to help sell the effect. For instance, a breakaway clock can have a cast plaster case with a real clock face attached to the outside and real guts inside. They will spill out when the case is broken. Tie them together with fishing line to prevent them from scattering too far on stage; the real parts are reused for every new clock.

For a softer and crumblier prop, mix plaster with Durham's Water Putty.

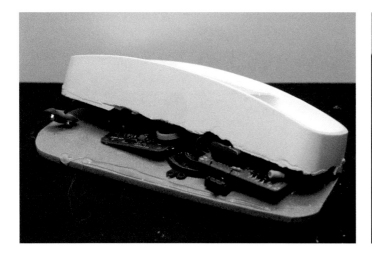

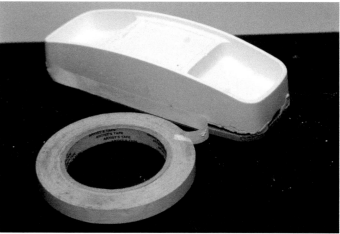

Figures 8.9, 8.10, and 8.11: A plaster cast was made in a mold of a phone receiver. Real phone parts were loosely attached to a wooden base. A new plaster cast was adhered to the base for every performance. *The Book of Grace*, The Public Theater, 2010. Designed by Eugene Lee.

Wax

Paraffin wax (or canning wax) can be cast and broken. Wax cups can also hold cool liquids. Heat the wax in a double boiler until melted. You can cast it in a plaster or silicone rubber mold.

For a plaster mold, soak the mold in cold water before casting. Fill the mold with wax and swill it around to coat all the sides. Invert the mold and let the excess wax drain out. You can do further coats to make it thicker.

For a silicone rubber mold, fill the entire mold with wax. After the wax cools for about an hour, turn the mold over and let the excess drain out.

Wax is fairly brittle, but it does not have any sharp edges when broken. Plus, the pieces can be melted down and reused repeatedly. You can tint melted wax with candle dye or bits of crayon. You can even paint finished wax with acrylics.

For extra durability, embed tissue paper into the wax while it is still melted. Use multiple pieces to control where the prop breaks; the gaps between the pieces of tissue paper will break the easiest.

Greenware and Bisqueware

Water-based clay can be cast into breakaways. Air-drying clay may become too hard when dry. It can be made into a liquid slip and poured into a mold. The disadvantage of clay is it becomes crumbly when broken, and the pieces will be ground into the floor as actors walk over them. However, this crumbliness may be preferred when sharp edges absolutely must be avoided.

Clay is cast through slip casting in a plaster mold. With **slip casting**, the mold is filled with liquid clay. The clay solidifies over time. It becomes solid from the outside in. Wait a few minutes until the piece is as thick as you want, then pour the excess clay out.

You can also roll clay into sheets and press them into the sides of a mold.

Let the clay sit in the mold for a few hours until it can be removed without losing its shape. Demold and let dry overnight. A drying rack or dehumidifier can help speed the process, but do not blow air directly on the piece or it will dry unevenly and crack. Clay cannot have any water in it if you want to fire it.

The plaster needs to be completely dry when casting. If you are doing multiple casts in a day, the plaster may still be wet from the previous cast, so the next one will take longer to reach your desired thickness.

When a clay piece dries, it is known as **greenware**. Greenware can be sealed and painted and used as a breakaway. It does not make any sound when broken and quickly turns to dust. It also does not have sharp edges when it breaks. However, it is a great option if you do not have access to a kiln.

The first firing of a piece, before the glaze is applied, is known as a bisque firing. The resulting ceramic piece is called **bisqueware**. Bisqueware is less fragile and can be painted, but is still more easily broken than completely fired clay.

You can find vendors online who will sell bisqueware in bulk. If you only need a few pieces, you can find bisqueware at those "paint your own" ceramic craft stores.

Commercial bisque firing is usually done at a high temperature (minimum of 1751°F or 956°C) which results in pieces that are harder to break. It is better to fire greenware yourself at a lower temperature, such as cone 018 (around 1353°F or 734°C), to get a piece that breaks easily and without sharp edges. Since few prop shops have their own kilns, a local potter or school can be enlisted to fire pieces for you.

You can apply underglaze colors before firing. Otherwise, the fired piece can be painted and decorated. If the piece needs holes drilled or lines scored, it is best to do this before firing.

Sugar Glass and Isomalt

For breakaway glass and other clear items, special materials are needed. Sugar glass has historically been the cheapest option. It is incredibly finicky to work with, however, and becomes very sticky and flexible in a humid environment.

Though many prop masters avoid sugar glass for its myriad problems, I include the recipe here for completeness:

- 2 cups water
- 1 cup white corn syrup
- 3 ½ cups sugar
- ¼ teaspoon cream of tartar

Mix thoroughly, then place in a pot and heat until it begins boiling. You can sprinkle a bit of salt into the mixture to make it less shiny. Let it continue to boil until the temperature reaches 300°F (149°C). Once the temperature has been reached, pour it immediately.

Isomalt is a sugar substitute preferred by confectioners for sugar sculpture for the same reasons that we should prefer it for making breakaways. It does not crystallize like regular sugar (sucrose) and it resists humidity better. It is easy to work with and can produce clear and glossy casts. It is available already cooked in sticks or nibs, or can be bought in an uncooked powdered form. Larger shards (or failed castings) can be remelted.

Cooked isomalt can be liquefied in a microwave and then poured. Uncooked isomalt is cooked in a stainless-steel saucepan or pot. Add just enough water to make it look like wet sand. Heat it to at least 340°F (170°C) using a candy thermometer to keep track of the temperature. When it reaches its temperature, remove it from the heat and plunge the base of the pan into cold water to stop it from cooking. Keep the pot in an oven which is heated to 275–300°F (135–148°C) to keep it in a liquid state as you pour your casts throughout the day.

Liquid isomalt can be poured into a silicone mold that is lightly greased or sprayed with vegetable oil. For best results, preheat the mold. The longer the isomalt is kept in a molten state, the fewer bubbles the final piece will have.

Figures 8-12 and 8-13: Uncooked isomalt starts out as white powder and becomes a clear liquid as it is heated.

Impurities will discolor the isomalt. Use only distilled water. Pots and utensils should be stainless steel or silicone.

Store the finished props in an airtight container with silica gel packets to keep moisture out. Stored properly like this, they will remain crystal clear for months or even years.

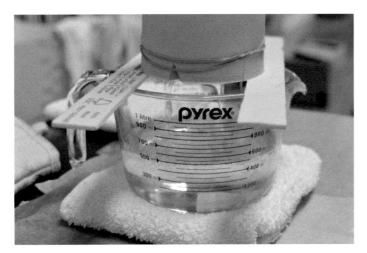

Figures 8-14, 8-15, and 8-16: Fill the mold with isomalt. Wait a few minutes for the isomalt to cool around the mold and form a shell, then turn it upside and let the excess liquid drain out. The isomalt remains molten for a bit, so leave it upside down. If you leave it on its side, it will sag and one side will be thicker than the other, and if you turn it right-side up, the bottom may become too thick to break. It will reach a point where it is no longer a liquid but has not achieved its candy-shell hardness; you can use a sharp knife which has been heated to trim all the drips off the top and make a clean edge.

Transparent Breakaway Resins

Picco resin (or clear brittle polymer, CBP) is the go-to material used in films for breakaway bottles and windows. One brand name is Ultra Breakaway Prop Polymer. It melts to a liquid between 250 and 300°F (121°C–149°C). Larger pieces can be melted down and reused. It is not edible like sugar glass.

These are hot, sticky liquids, so wear leather gloves, a leather apron, and a face shield to protect yourself from splashes and spills.

Picco resin is a blend of Piccolastic 100 Resin, which is flexible, and Piccotex D100 Resin, which is brittle. A mix of one part Piccolastic to one part Piccotex is recommended for most applications. Some prop shops will use up to three parts Piccolastic to one part Piccotex for a window pane. Feel free to experiment if you want it to break differently or produce different size shards. The proportions affect the color and opacity, as well as the stiffness and fragility.

One pound of Piccolastic melts down to 16.5fl oz (500mL), and one pound of Piccotex melts down to 18.5fl oz (550mL). A large whiskey bottle needs about 7fl oz (200mL) to make.

Melt the resins together in a covered electric saucepan or a pot on an electric stove top. A double boiler with cooking oil in the bottom will also help you reach the correct temperature.

Be sure the resins mix evenly together. Do not stir the mixture too much, or you will trap air bubbles inside. Let it melt for one hour. The mixture will melt around 350°F (177°C), but heating it to 400°F (204°C) will allow you to pour it without trapping too many air bubbles. Overheating it will discolor the final piece.

Carefully pour the melted resin onto your pre-heated silicone rubber mold. Pour slowly to avoid trapping air bubbles in the cast. Be sure your mold is level as it cools.

When cool, carefully peel the mold away from the breakaway piece. Keep it wrapped or padded while storing. Remember, if it breaks ahead of time or comes out imperfect, just melt the pieces down and try again. However, repeated reheating of pieces will eventually darken the mix.

Translucent resin dyes can be added for color.

The pots or pans you use for picco resin should never be used for anything else, nor should the stirring utensils you use.

SMASH! Plastic by Smooth-On is a two-part resin that cures to a clear plastic which shatters and crumbles like glass when broken. No heating is involved: just mix the two liquids in the correct proportion, and pour it into the mold before it cures to a solid.

It is a challenge to pour it thin enough to look realistic but thick enough not to break while handling. Usually the pieces need to be around ¼" (6mm) thick. Smash Plastic has a tendency to trap bubbles while it cures. The room needs to be well ventilated and the temperature above 68°F (20°C) for it to cure.

Smash Plastic can cause very bad reactions to anyone exposed to it while curing. Any exposed skin or skin covered in light fabric can break out into a rash from the fumes as it cures (even if it is off-gassing inside a spray booth). Far too many prop builders I know have had severe allergic reactions to this, even when they thought they were using it safely.

Smooth-On Rubber Glass is a clear silicone rubber which realistically resembles shards of broken glass after it crumbles. As a rubber, these pieces are flexible and do not have sharp edges, making them safe to handle by actors. However, it does not shatter on impact or make a sound when it breaks.

Glasses made from plastic resins should not be drunk from. While the shards from sugar glass and breakaway resins are not as dangerous as real glass, they can still be sharp and splintery. Be careful!

Breaking Pane of Window Glass

You can make a mold for a window pane in one of two ways. Use heat-resistant silicone rubber to make the mold from a real window pane you are trying to duplicate, or from a sheet good that is the same size and thickness you are trying to achieve. You will also need a flat rigid surface for the mold to sit on, as a thin sheet of silicone will not support itself.

You can also make a mold by clamping four pieces of angle iron around the sides of a flat sheet of material. Use a thick sheet of metal like aluminum or stainless steel that can be preheated. If you do not have a large enough plate of metal, a sheet of smooth plywood or Masonite will suffice. It should be thick enough to remain rigid without support. Cover the surface with aluminum foil or cellophane and line the edges of the angle iron with Teflon tape to prevent the resin from sticking. Be sure the foil or cellophane are perfectly smooth and flat, as any wrinkles will add texture to your glass panel.

For both isomalt and picco resin, preheat your mold. If you have a silicone mold, place it on a flat plate that can withstand high temperatures, such as ¼″ aluminum. Regular baking sheets are not useful as they warp slightly when heated. Warm the mold on the plate in an oven for ten to 15 minutes. After pouring the pane, return the mold and plate to the oven for another 15 minutes. This resting period allows the air bubbles to rise to the surface and the casting material to spread out evenly. If you pour your casting material onto a room temperature mold, it will begin hardening before it can flow to all the edges.

> You will be far less stressed if you make a window out of several smaller panes rather than one large pane. The mullions can be made of balsa wood so they break as well. You can have a whole bunch of small panes ready to go if one of them breaks before the show. Large panes are much more difficult to make, and you will probably only be able to make one at a time.

Buying Breakaways

You can buy breakaway glasses and bottles in a variety of shapes. They may seem expensive, but if you do the math, the materials and labor for making your own can often cost more. Plus, many shops are not adequately equipped to deal with the toxicity of breakaway plastic resins. Unless you need a custom shape or a vast quantity, buying breakaways is often the best option.

These breakaways are likely made of a plastic resin. While they can hold a small amount of room temperature liquid, actors should not drink from them.

The Old Switcheroo

Any item that needs to perform actions beforehand, such as furniture which is sat on or cups that are drunk from, can be difficult to make both functional and breakable. Your life will become so much easier if you can convince the director to stage the scene so there is an opportunity for the prop to be switched with an identical breakaway immediately prior to the destructive moment. This is common practice in even the most professional theatres with large budgets.

Cleanup

The problem with many breakaways is what happens in the aftermath. If you have shards of sugar glass, clay, or some other material all over the floor, you will now hear actors crunching over them until the end of the show. You will probably want to work out some moment where crew can clean them up, or stage it so the bulk lands on a rug or piece of scenery that can be struck offstage.

nine

smoke and fire

The use of real flame on stage is highly dependent on your venue, its location, and the local fire department. Laws differ by country, state, and municipality. You can have different regulations within suburbs of the same city, or even within the same venue, depending on which fire marshal shows up that day. Ultimately, the fire marshal has the final say, regardless of what you think the laws allow. Most performing-arts venues develop a relationship with their local fire department so they can become familiar with what they need to do, which will allow for some consistency in policies and procedures over time.

Permits and inspections can be needed for something as simple as a single match on stage; your theatre may even have a complete ban on any live flame. More complicated flame effects involving fuel like propane require the kind of hands-on training that cannot be conveyed in a book, so I will not discuss them here. I will briefly touch on simple flame effects such as matches, lighters, cigarettes, and candles, but keep in mind these may require a permit and inspection by the fire department, as well as additional safety procedures both before and during the production.

The rest of this chapter is devoted to fake fire and smoke effects which are achieved without the use of real flame.

Real Fire

If you have an open flame or anything burning in front of an audience, you have a **flame effect**. This can include matches, cigarettes, candles, burning paper, and even propane fires or other fuels.

These differ from pyrotechnic effects because they need the oxygen from the room air to burn. In a **pyrotechnic effect**, the fuel is compounded with an oxidizer and does not need air to burn.

In most jurisdictions, you need a licensed pyrotechnician present during a live performance with pyrotechnics. In some cases, the pyrotechnician needs to physically handle all the effects, rather than being able to pass them off to an actor to handle. Unless your theatre has a licensed pyrotechnician on staff who can commit to being at every performance, you will need to hire one for the show, which can be a huge expense.

Obtaining a pyrotechnic license often involves three years of assisting a licensed pyrotechnician. You should only use these effects if you have this kind of hands-on training, so I will not describe their use in this book.

In some jurisdictions, even flash paper and flash cotton requires a licensed pyrotechnician onsite. Do your homework before using any commercially available products. Just because you do not need a license to purchase a product does not mean you do not need one to use it in front of an audience.

Real Candles

Not all candles are the same. For stage use, you want candles that drip as little as possible. It could take some experimentation to find which supplier or store has the candles in the size, shape, and price you need with the least amount of dripping. Camper lantern candles are usually fairly dripless (though no candle is going to be completely dripless).

Soaking the candles in a salt water bath overnight and then letting them dry out before going on stage will help minimize dripping.

Fire ribbon, or fire paste, is a fire starter that you squeeze out from a tube (like toothpaste). It is sold in

Figure 9-1: Double wick candles have two wicks in the center. They are used in films because they burn more brightly and do not accidentally extinguish as easily as regular candles. You can find a few shops that sell them, though most places custom make them, so allow plenty of lead time when ordering them.

camping, hiking, and hunting stores. A very small amount is used on candles to help them light more quickly and easily.

Real Lighters and Matches

You can find two basic styles of lighters. One I call the "Bic" style, and the other I call the "Zippo" style. Fire marshals prefer the Bic style, and in some venues they are the only type of lighter allowed. A Bic lighter is **self-extinguishing**; the actor needs to hold the button down to keep the flame lit. If they drop it, the flame will go out before the lighter hits the ground. On a Zippo lighter, the flame continues to burn even if no one is touching it, making it a greater fire hazard.

You can find two types of matches: safety matches, and strike anywhere. **Safety matches** need to be lit on the special striking plate that comes on the box. A **strike anywhere match** can be lit on any rough surface, such as a piece of sandpaper. We often hide pieces of sandpaper all over the set for the actor to use. Directors usually prefer strike anywhere matches because they tend to be more reliable; as the striking plate for safety matches gets used up, they become more difficult to light. However, strike anywhere matches have gotten particularly tricky to find. It is rare to find a local source, so you need to order them online, and they usually need to be ground shipped because of their flammability, so do not expect to be able to overnight them.

The head on a safety match is a solid color, usually red or blue, though newer ones are green. The head on a strike anywhere match is a single color with a white tip.

Fire Safety

Any use of flame on stage requires careful planning, absolute consistency in performances, and multiple options for extinguishing the effect. Fires in theatres still kill dozens and even hundreds of people a year. The main culprit is people who think "it can't happen here," and all the rules and regulations just get in the way. My personal belief is that you should avoid the use of actual flame whenever possible. If a scene or effect absolutely requires it, be prepared to spend the time and money to do it safely.

A consistent effect requires a **fire plan**. This will be a written document kept throughout the run of the show and shared with the fire marshal. A fire plan typically includes:

- A list of all open flame and pyrotechnic effects and their ingredients.
- A stage plan layout including the timing, location, and duration of each effect.
- The costume the actor is wearing and the materials of everything else in the vicinity (five feet or so) of the effect.
- Where the combustible materials will be stored.

Getting the proper permits can take a few weeks for approval, so start early. Be prepared to demonstrate the effect to the fire marshal.

A **fire watch** is staffed with a crew member trained to use a fire extinguisher. They need a direct path to the fire effect and should be stationed as close to it as possible They absolutely *cannot have any other duties* while the flame effect is in play. Ideally, they will remain present for several minutes before and after the effect as well. Their job is to rush out on stage immediately to extinguish the effect should anything go wrong.

You may need two fire watch stations: one on either side of the stage, or one for the entrance and one for the exit of a moving effect.

All materials within a certain distance of the effect (typically around 5 feet or 1.5m) must be noncombustible or treated with flame retardant. For moving effects, the entire path must be made flame retardant.

If you ever have a vehicle on stage, note that many fire marshals do not like their tanks to be full of fuel and oil. Be ready to drain them, and if they need to move, rig up a different method of propulsion, such as electrical.

Flame Retardant

Flame retardant does not mean a material will not burn or be damaged in a fire. What it means is that the fire will spread slowly on it and the flame will self-extinguish. It will still burn if continually subjected to an ignition source. No material is truly "fireproof."

Depending on the material of your prop, you can use different coatings or treatments to make it flame retardant. Rosco has a line of Flamex flame-retardant chemicals for some of the more common materials. Another brand is Inspecta-Shield. They do leave a noticeable coating on the object. For solid wood, it is not really noticeable, but for fabrics, it can change how they drape and handle. If you wash or wet them, the salts will lift and form a visible ring. Flame retardants can also be mixed into paint before being applied.

Use naturally or inherently flame-retardant materials to make your life easier. Metal like steel and aluminum, plaster, drywall, and glass are all flame retardant or noncombustible. Props made from fiberglass are only flame resistant if you use a flame-resistant resin. Wool and some cottons may be flame retardant. Some synthetic fabrics are available in inherently flame-resistant forms. You can find fire-retardant treated lumber and plywood (*not* the same as pressure-treated lumber); otherwise, any wood needs to be coated. Most plastics are not flame retardant, with the exception of PVC

Depending on your location and venue, the testing or treating of flame retardancy may need to be performed by a certified individual.

(vinyl) and plastics containing PVC (such as Kydex). Polystyrene foam is not flame retardant.

Smoke Effects

Most theatrical smoke is not actually smoke: that involves burning, which is something we want to avoid. However, I do want to mention **smoke emitter matches** before getting into purely theatrical effects. These are used for testing and inspecting air ducts in buildings. You light them like a regular match and immediately blow out the flame; they will then emit a non-toxic smoke for ten to 20 seconds. These do involve a brief flame, so can be regulated like other flame effects. However, many fire marshals are happy with them because the flame is immediately extinguished.

Otherwise, the smoke effects we use on stage fall into several categories: theatrical fog, dry ice, powder puffs, and steam or mist. These will each be discussed in turn.

Foggers

Modern theatrical foggers typically heat a glycol-based fluid to create fog. Always use the fog fluid intended for your machine. Do not mix and match with other types of fog fluid or experiment with homemade chemicals.

The fog machine can be placed right where you need the effect, or the fog can be ducted to another location through tubes and hoses. Small fans may be needed to move the fog through the tube. You can also use multiple hoses to divert the fog to several locations.

Figure 9-2: A small fogger was used to deliver a plume of smoke from the top of this clock. *The Pajama Game*, The Wirtz Center, 2013. Photo courtesy of Alec Thorne.

If the prop is too small to hold your fogger, stick a fogger inside a piece of furniture or scenery where the prop will sit while it smokes. Drill a hole near it (upstage if possible so it remains hidden). The fog should look like it is coming from that thing.

The Tiny Fogger line contains some of the smallest theatrical foggers, with 4 inches being the smallest one available. Unfortunately, they also cost several thousand dollars.

Magician suppliers have tiny handheld foggers that can fit up your sleeve. Two of the most well known are Pure Smoke and Vapr. These essentially consist of an air pump hooked up to an e-cigarette. They are small enough to fit inside a handheld clothes iron to make fake puffs of steam. Though the amount of fog they create is limited, they are cheap enough (in comparison to tiny theatrical foggers) for you to have two or three inside your prop.

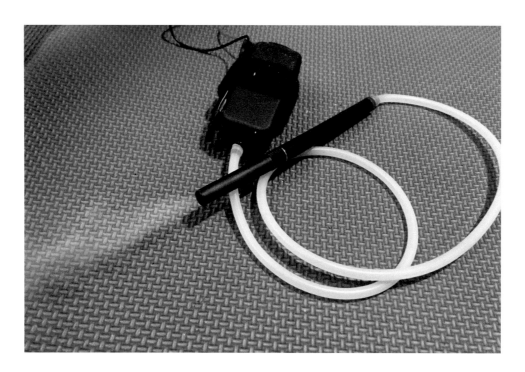

Figure 9-3: A magician's handheld fogger.

Hair Spray and Haze in a Can

Theatrical hazers use mineral oil to create a more general atmosphere throughout the theatre rather than concentrated clouds of fog. Props rarely uses hazers; however, "haze in a can" products use similar technology.

Brands like Fantasy FX "Haze in a can," Atmosphere Aerosol, Spray smoke, etc, can be found in magician supply stores, or film and photography suppliers. You can find similar cans of fake hairspray (also by Fantasy FX) designed specifically for the musical, *Hairspray*. Depending on the duration of the spray, one can may last anywhere from six to 30 performances. Combined with a lighting effect, you can also use these to simulate items such as blowtorches, flame throwers, and jet packs.

Another alternative is water facial spray, used for a quick refresher on a hot day. Some of it comes in containers similar to hairspray. It sprays like an aerosol, but it is only water. It is less cloudy than smoke in a can, but for a quick spritz, it is a convincing effect.

Figures 9-4 and 9-5: When using pretend hairspray, instruct the actors to aim just upstage of their head. The haze will leave an oily residue if they spray it directly on their hair.

What Does Equity Allow?

The unions which cover performers have regulations governing the use of atmospheric effects and chemical fog. One we deal with frequently in theatre is Actors' Equity. You are not allowed to subject Equity performers to an excess of fog or haze as stipulated in their guidelines. This requires taking samples of the air during show conditions while the atmospheric effects are in use.

The concentration of fog is tested with an approved aerosol monitor, like the Thermo pDR 1000. You also need to be familiar with all the Equity guidelines. The machines cost several thousand dollars to purchase, but you can usually rent them for $50–100 a day.

Equity has tested some of the most common fog machines and formulas, and published guidelines on acceptable use based on the duration they are used and the distance from the performers. By following these Time and Distance Guidelines, a theatre can use certain fog effects without having to do their own costly testing.

For example, using the CITC Fantasy FX Professional Haze (fake hairspray) for ten seconds keeps the actor within

acceptable exposure limits. Using it for 15 seconds will put the air within a 2-foot radius beyond the acceptable exposure limits for two seconds. An Equity actor would need to avoid the vicinity of the hairspray for two seconds (a tricky proposition, since this particular effect is handheld). These guidelines also list a few e-cigarette and other small fog devices.

Some managers refer to the list of devices in the Time and Distance Guidelines as "Equity-approved" foggers. This is not strictly true. Any fog machine or e-cigarette can be used if you are able to afford the testing process and it passes. And even if you only stick to devices listed in the Time and Distance Guidelines, Equity can still request a test, which must be fulfilled if you want to use the device. This is highly unlikely, but still possible.

Other unions have their own guidelines. AGMA, which covers opera singers and some dance companies, has much stricter guidelines.

Liquid and solid air effects, like dry ice and liquid nitrogen, do not fall under these guidelines, and are usually the only style of fog allowed when all others are banned.

Dry Ice

Dry ice is frozen carbon dioxide. As it warms up, it sublimates, meaning it transforms directly from a solid to a gas without melting to a liquid in between. The resulting gas is so cold it causes the water vapor in the air to condense and make mist. Eventually, it will warm up to room temperature and cease to make fog.

To make instant fog, dry ice is dropped into hot water. You will recognize dry ice fog because it is heavier than air, so it flows downward. You may be able to mitigate this with a fan, or by filling an area from below.

Five pounds (2.27kg) of dry ice in four to five gallons (15 to 19L) of hot water will make a large amount of fog for five to ten minutes. Lots of small pieces of dry ice will make a larger amount of fog than the same amount of

Figure 9-6: A small piece of dry ice was dropped into this chalice full of hot water.

dry ice in one large piece. It also cools the water down more quickly. The water can be continually heated with a hot plate, electric skillet, or other device. The hotter the water, the more fog is created. If the pieces of dry ice are too small, they may react violently when touching hot water, so be careful.

Full-stage effects use large dry ice machines, but props usually just need a plastic cup or small tub of water with a few pieces of dry ice. The ice can be dropped in by a crew member wearing gloves immediately before the prop comes onstage, or triggered onstage by the actor. No one should touch the dry ice with bare hands. Instead, you will need to build a mechanism that can drop the ice on cue. A mesh tea ball is a handy way to hold and handle a small piece of dry ice.

Be sure to rehearse the scenes with dry ice carefully so you can determine how much dry ice is needed, what size the pieces should be, and when to drop it in the water. It is important to practice all the dry ice effects in real time as they would appear in the show. If you have multiple dry ice moments, the water may have cooled down from the first moment and not heated all the way up again by the second moment, resulting in less fog. In these cases, you would need some hot water standing by to replenish your tub, or just drop the dry ice into a second tub.

When dry ice is dropped into water, it will splash and bubble out of the container. Be sure you have some way of containing or channeling the water that splashes out (a few towels around the tub may be all you need). The vapor from the dry ice will dampen anything it touches, so make a plan to control the slipperiness of any floor areas. Keep it away from items that are not water resistant.

Dry ice fills the room with carbon dioxide. Without adequate ventilation, anyone in the room will be deprived of oxygen. It is particularly dangerous if an actor is lying on the floor under a cloud of dry ice fog, or if the fog pours down into the orchestra pit or audience seating. You must have adequate ventilation in your theatre to use these effects. Use strategically placed fans to direct the fog away from problem areas. Avoid having actors lie down in the fog or have fog so deep it covers small children.

Dry ice does not last long so do not buy it too far in advance of when you need it. You can buy it from many grocery and general merchandise stores. Some businesses will deliver larger quantities to your theatre, such as catering companies and beverage distributors. Store it in an ice chest or cooler. It is so cold, that if you store it in a regular freezer, the freezer will turn off. Do not store it in an airtight container because the gas expands as it sublimates.

Do not touch dry ice with your bare hands or skin; wear heavy canvas or leather gloves. It will burn your bare skin. Wear goggles when breaking apart the ice.

I have never run across any props people using liquid nitrogen for effects. It is tricky to obtain and has a high potential for danger. It is best used by experienced professionals for larger-scale effects.

Powder Puffs

As we saw in the chapter on pneumatics, you can use corn starch or other powders for a quick puff of smoke. Connect a squeeze bulb with some tubing to a chamber filled with cornstarch.

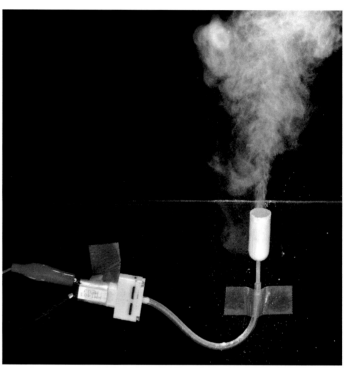

Figure 9.8: Micro air pumps, typically used for aquariums, are quick ways of making electrically triggered puffs of cornstarch. They are not very quiet, but require fewer parts than a pneumatic system.

Figure 9.7: In this funerary urn trick, a momentary button was concealed so the urn would hit it when it fell. The button triggered a two-way solenoid valve, which blew a small pile of cornstarch into the air. *Twelfth Night*, The Public Theater, 2009.

You can hide the chamber and tubing in a goblet and put the squeeze bulb in the base. This is an easy way to make an effect where a puff of smoke is produced when a magic elixir is added to the goblet.

If you can time the puff of smoke to trigger at the same time as a camera flash unit, you can imitate an old-timey camera flash without the use of combustible materials.

For darker powder, use charcoal dust. Mix cornstarch and charcoal dust together for a custom shade.

Steam

Prop builders adapt any number of common devices to produce steam, from travel steamers to electric tea kettles. You can run tubing from them to hide the steamer.

Another group of devices used to create "steam" are ultrasonic mist makers. You can find them used in ponds for making mist or in humidifiers for raising the humidity in a room. They also sell them for special effects, like DJ equipment or Halloween. They sit under a small layer of water, and make mist by vibrating the water very quickly. The mist is just water vapor rather than potentially toxic chemicals. They need to sit still, though, so they cannot be used on props that move around a lot.

Figure 9.9: An ultrasonic humidifier produces visible mist from water without the use of heat.

How to Make an Actor's Breath Visible to Simulate Cold Temperatures

This comes up frequently, but there has yet to be a safe solution that is visible to the audience. The best solution is for the actor to palm an e-cigarette and sneak a quick drag, but that is not always possible. If the director continues to insist on a solution, you can claim that an actor's breath is not a prop.

Safety of Fog and Smoke Effects

The risks and health concerns are different for each of the four types of atmospheric effects: glycols (including glycerin), mineral oil, cryogenic solids and gases, and water.

Glycols and glycerin are used in most foggers as well as e-cigarettes. They cause irritation in the nose, throat, and lungs if too much is inhaled. They may even cause or worsen asthma.

Mineral oil is found in hazers and haze in a can. While it is inert and safe to ingest, that does not make it safe to inhale. It will also cause upper respiratory irritation if too much is inhaled. Mineral oil is no longer used in nose drops and medicine for children because if it is accidentally inhaled, it can cause chemical pneumonitis (or chemical pneumonia). While the amount of mineral oil in haze is minute, the particles are extremely small, so they can be inhaled into the deepest parts of the lung and remain there for years, building up over time.

The American Conference of Governmental Industrial Hygienists (ACGIH) set a limit of 10mg/m3 for glycerin mist to protect workers from upper respiratory irritation. Glycols have no official limit for exposure. However, Equity has conducted a study by ENVIRON International Corporation and the Mount Sinai School of Medicine to determine maximum exposure levels to actors of these atmospheric effects.

	Peak	Time-weighted average (8-hour day)
Glycol	40mg/m3	–
Glycerin (glycerol)	50mg/m3	10mg/m3
Mineral oil	25mg/m3	5mg/m3

Even if you do not have to deal with Equity, these exposure levels and the time and distance guidelines for various fog devices are good to follow to avoid risking the health of your cast and crew.

These guidelines are developed for healthy, working adults. Young children, the elderly, and people with respiratory problems, particularly asthma, can be in danger at much lower levels. Avoid subjecting your audience to these effects wherever possible.

Cryogenic solids and liquids include dry ice and liquid nitrogen. When they warm up to room temperature, they create fog and mist. The gas itself is not toxic: it is the same gas we already breathe. However, it elevates the amount of that gas in the room, pushing out the oxygen. Unless used in a large, well-ventilated area, you run the risk of oxygen deprivation.

No dust is good for a person to inhale. When we talk about dust effects in this chapter, they are meant to be small, momentary effects. Whenever possible, the effect should be prevented from blowing into the actor's face. Certain types of dust are worse than others, and should be avoided. Mineral dusts like talc, Fuller's earth, and vermiculite can damage the lungs and cause diseases similar to those from asbestos exposure. Organic dusts can be explosive in high concentrations (look up "grain silo explosions" to see examples). Do not use them in conjunction with live flame. They can cause irritation and lead to allergies. Wood dust is particularly sensitizing and toxic. Wheat flour can lead to allergies and asthma, and can be immediately harmful to actors with gluten allergies.

Any very fine fiber like asbestos can damage the lungs. You may be tempted to use flocking powder for a colored smoke effect, but it should be avoided.

I used cornstarch in the examples in this book. Again, the effects are small, intermittent, and kept away from the actors' faces. Of course, the use of larger pieces of debris without dust, such as crumbled cork or foam beads, will almost eliminate any air pollution.

Water mist and steam effects can be among the safest effects since our bodies are designed to breathe wet air. However, only clean water should be used; distilled water is highly recommended. Any dirt, dust, or other contaminants in the water will end up in your lungs. Standing water left for long periods in the machines will grow bacteria and mold, which you do not want to breathe in. Keep your machines as clean as possible, use fresh water as much as possible, and dry out all parts when you are finished using them.

You can lose a finger, an eye, and even a leg and still function within society. Your lungs, however, are needed every second of every day. Breathing glycol and mineral oil fog and haze over a long period of time can impair and damage your lungs. Use these effects only when absolutely necessary, and limit everyone's exposure as much as possible.

Flicker Candles

Candle flame can be simulated by using flame-shaped bulbs. You can find "flickering" flame bulbs at the hardware store, but these are often horrendous and fake.

Plenty of cheap tea-candle-style flicker lights can be ripped apart and integrated into props; some are so cheap they can be used as a consumable since they are cheaper than replacing bulbs and batteries.

You can also find battery-operated candles that can be "blown" out. The only downside is they can accidentally be blown back on again. They are triggered by the sound of the breath, so can be triggered by loud claps or when dropped.

The most realistic flicker bulbs are theatrical brands such as The Candle Lite or Rosco Flicker Candles.

Some of these flicker bulbs or flicker LEDs can be improved by building a fake flame over them. A dab of hot glue over the top can easily be shaped into a flame, and it will glow from the light. Colored gel, oiled tissue paper, or Mylar can be cut and arranged over the top as well.

For lights run from the light board, you can have a flickering effect programmed in, so the prop itself doesn't need its own flicker circuit or mechanism. You can also find solutions which let you build and fine-tune all sorts of random flicker and flash lighting effects without having to write a program from scratch. For instance,

Figure 9-11: A popular non-theatrical brand is Luminara, which comes in a variety of candle shapes and sizes. Luminara candles have a small flame-shaped piece of plastic which wiggles from a magnet, in addition to a light source. It gives a very realistic naked flame look from a short distance. If viewed from above, you can see the light source, so it is not good in spaces where the audience is close to but higher than the stage. These were developed by Disney and are the most realistic fake candles you can find. Some versions come with their own remote. If you wanted to introduce your own remote or hook them to a wireless dimmer, it would take some gutting and resoldering of parts. Inside, you will find the magnet runs on about 3V and the lights run on about 2V.

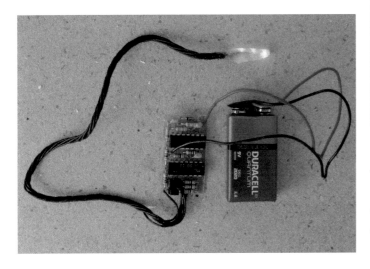

Figure 9-10: The Candle Lite kit from City Theatrical lets you put a flickering flame-shaped incandescent light in any fixture you can fit it in. All it needs is a 9V battery and a switch if you want one.

Figure 9-12: The LightLi brand candle is similar to the Luminara, but it is also available with a screw base for attaching to AC light fixtures.

Figure 9-13: A fluorescent starter wired in series with an incandescent bulb creates a random flickering effect. Watch the companion video to see the flicker in action.

RC4 Dimmers come with a Wireless Flkr Effects Engine, while the Flickermaster DMX8 is a standalone unit.

If you have multiple candles around the stage, say a few candelabra and some chandeliers, it can be very distracting and almost seizure-inducing for all of them to have flicker bulbs. Save the flicker for the hero props or for the special "candle moments." For a great mass of candles, you can get away with regular flame-shaped bulbs. If they are on a dimmer, your lighting designer can even program them to have a slight organic pulse rather than just a steady glow. A real candle in a stationary fixture does not really flicker that much. A kerosene flame should not flicker at all.

Burning Coals and Embers

The hardest part about making a fake fire is the flames. Often, the best effects use a combination of smoke plus flickering light.

Burning coals and embers can be simulated by placing fake coals and firewood on top of chicken wire or transparent plastic. Beneath this are placed either colored lights, or lights with colored gels. Oranges and yellows work best; pure red does not make a realistic looking glow. The front and sides can be disguised with more wood, coals, andirons, or other fireplace decoration, or the lights can be sunk below the deck inside the fireplace.

The lights can be programmed to have a flickering glow from the light board.

For a cheap standalone flicker effect, wire a fluorescent starter in series with a 120 VAC bulb (incandescent, halogen, or LED). Multiple bulbs should each have their own starter; otherwise, every bulb will flicker with the same rhythm rather than randomly. Different types are indicated by FS (fluorescent starter) and a number. Use FS-2 or FS-5 for these effects; an FS-4 will not work.

Figures 9-14 and 9-15: Clear sea glass can be painted black. It looks like solid coals until lit from beneath with orange light.

Figure 9-16: A campfire made from acrylic ice cubes, colored gels, and lights. *As You Like It*, The Public Theater, 2012. Photo courtesy of Jay Duckworth.

Glowing coals can be made by dusting acrylic ice or sea glass with black spray paint. Place it in a pile and hide some orange or red lights underneath. When these lights are off, it looks like burnt coals. When the lights are on, it glows like real embers.

Fabric Fire with Fan

You can buy already existing silk flame effects, from the expensive but realistic Le Flame units by Theatre Effects, to the cheap Halloween store units.

The cheap ones of course look cheap. The base can usually be covered over to look more realistic. They are usually pretty dim, so only work well in dark scenes. The motors can be very loud with no way to deaden the noise, which is why many prop masters avoid them.

Computer fans, often called **muffin fans**, are your best bet for smaller flames. They are compact, have holes for mounting, and usually run on 12VDC. Some (though not all) can be especially quiet.

A **squirrel cage blower** sucks air in through the sides and blows it out of a single exhaust hole. Sometimes a regular fan can create a weird vortex or abnormal airflow pattern depending on how it is positioned within the prop; a squirrel cage ensures the air is blown in a straight line out of the exhaust.

You can also cover a square fan with a circular cutout that blocks the corners where the weird downdrafts occur. You may also need to cover the fan with a piece of mesh to prevent the silk from falling between the fan blades when the fan is turned off.

Use the lightest silk you can find. China silk, also known as *habotai*, is what we think of when we think of theatrical silk. It is measured in momme weight, with higher numbers being thicker. You can easily find 5mm,

and with some hunting, you may find 4.5mm and even 4mm. You may also use silk gauze, which comes as thin as 3mm. Most of this comes undyed, so you will need to dye it all yourself. Luckily, silk dyes pretty easily, and splotchy mistakes will just add to the effect.

Use small pieces of silk anchored to wire. To determine the length of the flames you need, cut the pieces while the fans are running so they are just long enough to rise and fall realistically. If they are too long, they will never rise completely, and too short will just flap comically.

The more lights you can get shining onto the silk, the more realistic the effect will be. Some can be constant lights while others flicker or pulse. Again, a mix of orange and yellow light will look more realistic than red light.

A cheap torch effect can also be made using orange and yellow acetate, cellophane, or tissue

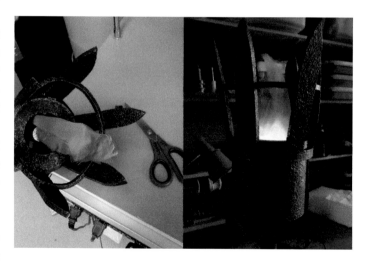

Figure 9-17: A silk flame torch. *The Lion, the Witch, and the Wardrobe*, Seattle Children's Theatre, 2016. Photos courtesy of Todd Peacock-Preston.

paper. The tissue paper can be oiled or varnished to make it translucent. The material can be crumpled and shaped to look like a flame, and then a light is hidden underneath which shines upwards through the flame. This is especially useful to make a handheld torch using a flashlight as the light source. Of course, the flame itself does not move, so the effect is not entirely realistic, but from a distance it will get the job done.

Oiled tissue paper can also be wrapped around a candle bulb to improve the appearance.

Steam Fire

A fairly realistic fake fire can be simulated with steam, mist, or fog, along with a few fans, and some lighting fixtures.

Direct the steam/fog/mist to a pipe with holes drilled along the top. It should be directed out upwards in a series of puffs. Shine lights upward into the steam. You may want to add a slight flickering effect for greater variety. For greatest realism, avoid red light and use deep orange instead. When possible, aim yellow light at the base of the steam and orange toward the top.

Any of the steam or mist sources mentioned earlier can be adapted for this. If the tubing is too long, the steam may cool and condense in the pipes or tubing before it exits. Mist and theatrical fog will not have this problem.

Explosions

You may need an explosion for faking black powder gun shots, cannons, or just general destruction. A good effect will have perfect timing between the puff of smoke, a lighting effect, a sound effect, and perhaps some additional flying debris or movement of the prop.

Cornstarch mixed with bits of flameproofed polystyrene foam beads, ground-up cork, or paper confetti can be fired from a small air cannon as described earlier. Heavier debris can be catapulted from a spring or elastic-powered device.

The lighting can come from a strobe, a camera flash, or just a very bright light that can be turned on and off quickly.

For a much more impressive effect, nearby props and set elements can be rigged to shake or fall down when the explosion occurs. These larger effects usually become a collaboration with the scenery department.

Smoking Onstage

The main types of smoking devices used by props people are real cigarettes, non-tobacco cigarettes, e-cigarettes, and puff cigarettes.

Because real and non-tobacco cigarettes involve burning, they are regulated or forbidden by your fire marshal. States and local jurisdictions may have additional regulations for the act of smoking onstage itself (real or simulated). You may find that real cigarettes are banned but non-tobacco ones are allowed; you may find that both are banned.

E-cigarettes can also be lumped in with smoking bans. In some venues, all three types of cigarettes are forbidden. Usually you will find e-cigarettes are allowed when real and non-tobacco ones are banned (though e-cigarettes are also regulated by Actors' Equity). In rare cases, a venue may ban e-cigarettes but allow non-tobacco (and even real) cigarettes. It is up to you and your superiors to be certain what is allowed for your production.

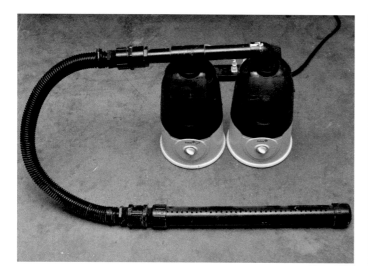

Figures 9-18 to 9-21: In this steam fire system, two ultrasonic humidifiers are connected with PVC pipe fittings. A hose runs from the humidifiers to a second piece of PVC with holes drilled along the length. The mist exits these holes. Lights placed behind and below the mist create the color and size of the flames. A small box fan at the top of the fireplace helps draw the mist upwards. A few craftily arranged logs help mask everything and direct the steam into realistic swirling patterns. For added realism, lights with a flicker sequence can be used.

Puff cigarettes use non-burning dust, and are allowed everywhere (except in high schools where even simulated smoking may be avoided).

Herbal cigarettes can still have some "medicinal" properties. Many theatres opt for cigarettes made from dried cocoa bean husks (not "coconut" as some actors mistakenly insist), which are sold as a smoking cessation aid. The choice of what type and brand of cigarette to use will always come down to the individual actor; if they do not like the taste, or feel it is harsh on their throat, you need to be prepared with a few other options. Years ago, many theatres swore by a lettuce-based cigarette called Bravo, which was also famous for being the brand used on the show *Mad Men*. Unfortunately, they have gone out of business.

You can also search for loose herbal blends if you need to make hand-rolled cigarettes or joints, or if your actor needs to roll a joint during a scene and smoke it. If you cannot find a loose blend you like, you can disassemble herbal cigarettes.

Nicotine-free *cigars* are nearly impossible to find since the wrapper itself is a tobacco leaf. You may occasionally find an enterprising props master who makes them, but they can be expensive.

An **e-cigarette**, or electronic cigarette, is a small device which vaporizes a mix of propylene glycol (PG) and vegetable glycerin (VG), along with nicotine and flavorings. You want to use nicotine-free liquid and find unflavored or neutral flavored liquid. They can create a pretty realistic alternative to cigarettes in venues where smoking or burning is not allowed.

An e-cigarette contains a base with all the electronics and a rechargeable battery, and a screw-on disposable cartridge containing the liquid. This typically goes where the filter of a real cigarette is located. The electronics are triggered when you inhale on the cartridge, and vapor enters your mouth almost immediately. For many e-cigarettes, the opposite end contains an LED which glows when it is active. If it is a red LED, it will look like the glowing ember of a cigarette from the audience. Many e-cigarettes will have a blue LED, which is not what you want for realism's sake.

One of the major problems with e-cigarettes is that they do not "smoke down." A real cigarette will get shorter as it is smoked, and burn down to the filter in about five to seven minutes. If you have an e-cigarette on stage for that amount of time, the audience will eventually realize it has not gotten any shorter. The director will need to block the scene so that the e-cigarette is only on briefly to establish the smoking, and then heads off stage or disappears into an ash tray.

If you need a "magical" cigarette, you can find e-cigarettes which are button activated rather than breath activated. Other vaping devices do not resemble cigarettes at all. These can produce much larger clouds of vapor, and some allow you to fill your own liquid so you do not have to buy disposable cartridges. You can use either propylene glycol (PG), vegetable glycerin (VG), or a mix of the two.

For an e-joint, you can roll a bit of tissue paper with some glue over an e-cigarette. Make the middle a little fatter than the ends and let the tissue extend past the lit end just a little bit. This creates an abnormally large joint which may not work when the audience is close.

You can find e-cigars, either disposable or rechargeable. They are fairly realistic, plus you can have a cigar onstage for a longer period of time without having to worry that it is not burning down shorter.

You can buy dedicated e-pipes, or stick a pipe bowl on the end of an existing e-cigarette.

You may have heard about e-cigarettes with exploding batteries. Any lithium-ion battery runs the risk of smoking, catching fire, or even exploding if it is pushed past what it was designed to do. News stories of exploding e-cigarettes involve user-modified units which were drawing more power than intended. Regular e-cigarettes, particularly the tried-and-true brands found in the Equity T&D Guidelines, are used by thousands of people each day without incident.

Figure 9-22: A Puff cigarette.

Some theatrical venues outright ban the use of e-cigarettes on stage. The laws surrounding e-cigarettes in general are in such flux nowadays that anything I write here may be completely outdated before the second edition of this book comes out. Many of the e-cigarette makers do not release the SDS of their liquids; these brands should be avoided.

A "Puff" cigarette, also known as a puff puff or joke cigarette, is a cigarette-shaped object filled with a small amount of dust (usually talcum powder or cornstarch). Rather than sucking, you blow, causing the dust to puff out. The end is typically made of red foil, so it looks like a glowing ember as it reflects the ambient light. Obviously, it does not smolder like a real cigarette, nor burn down in size. It takes a lot of acting to get these to look right; usually, you just need to give one or two puffs at the beginning of the scene to establish that it is a cigarette, and the rest of the time you can just gesture with the cigarette, pretend to ash it, or bring it to your mouth before starting another line of dialogue. The audience will rarely catch on that it is not a real cigarette.

These are the only option if real, herbal, and electronic cigarettes are all banned on your stage. They are also the safest since they involve no flame, and the actor never inhales anything.

The real ones are cheap enough that it is rarely worth making your own, but if you need one in an unusual size or style (like a puff cigar), they are easy to build.

Cut a drinking straw to length and wrap it in cigarette paper. Fill it with cornstarch and stuff a bit of cotton in each end to keep the powder inside. Glue a bit of red foil to the tip to hold the cotton in and give it a realistic "cherry."

A puff pipe is constructed similarly. Dust some cotton batting with corn starch and jam it inside the pipe. Put a small black mesh over the pipe bowl; it should be removable so you can add more powder to the batting as needed. It takes some experimentation to figure out how much batting to put in, how tight to fit it, and how much powder to include, but the end result is convincing enough on a stage where smoking or open flame is forbidden.

Theatrical Firearms

I will not discuss firearms in detail here because they introduce a whole slew of legalities and safety issues which are better covered in other books, like *The Theatrical Firearms Handbook* by the same publisher as this book. However, some blank ammunition is considered a pyrotechnic device, and requires licenses and safety considerations in addition to the gun-specific needs.

Black powder weapons are often simulated by building a dummy gun and using the powder puff effects discussed earlier in this chapter.

A **non-gun** is a type of prop made by Independent Studio Services (ISS). It has no moving parts other than the trigger, and is not considered a firearm, thus bypassing any need for permits or licenses. It fires an electric squib rather than an explosive powder, making them safer as well. They are expensive though.

Sparks

The eSquib Effects System (EES) from DSS Propulsion is an electric squib which creates no heat or risk of fire. They claim they can be used without a pyrotechnic license. They rent out the controllers and then you buy the squibs themselves.

Some prop builders have created sparks by running a Dremel wheel on a piece of flint. I am not sure whether this counts as an open flame, but it is similar to sparking a Bic lighter and should probably be demonstrated to your fire marshal just to be safe.

I have heard of theatres using an angle grinder and a piece of steel to produce sparks. This seems dangerous since it produces flying debris, and your audience is probably not wearing safety glasses. It is probably safer to have a licensed pyrotechnician provide you with a pyrotechnic effect if you really need a spark effect. Otherwise, you can build a lighting effect to imply a spark.

Sparklers

As far as I can tell, there is no sort of "fake" sparkler that exists without the use of heat or burning. The best you can hope for is a mix of tinsel or fiber optic strands that might look good from a distance. "Wedding" or "indoor" sparklers run colder than normal sparklers and are a bit safer to use on stage. These will definitely require approval from the Fire Marshal and possibly a pyrotechnics license to use.

Stoves

A working gas stove is often out of the question for most theatres. Instead, hide a small hot plate inside the burners. It needs to be hidden well, and up close it will be obvious it is an electric burner rather than a gas flame. Most venues allow a hot plate, though you will need to check about flame retarding the surrounding materials. Many fire marshals will want an easily accessible switch for a crew member to quickly kill its power in the event of an emergency.

You may also wish to retrofit a hot plate into an electric stove, since those typically require 220V and a hot plate will run off the more standard 110V (at least in the US).

ten

sound

Most theatres have a sound department responsible for all the sound effects and music in a play. A props department needs to work with them when a sound effect has to be integrated into a prop, such as with a working radio or a ringing phone. Other sound effects may need to be performed live, either by the prop itself or through an offstage device. These often become the responsibility of the props department because it goes beyond the sound department's skill set.

Mechanical Sound Effects

Long before sound effects could be played through speakers, the props department provided all sorts of live sound effects through a variety of interesting devices.

Some sound effects are better performed live. The quality of the sound may not be accurately recreated through a speaker; it may not gel with all the other ambient noise created by the actors interacting with the set; or the sound may need to react to the actors, which is challenging with a prerecorded bit. Finally, there are plays set in vintage radio studios or theatres where these vintage sound effect devices are themselves practical props.

What follows are a few of the most common practical sound effects, some of which have been used in theatres for centuries.

A **slapstick** consists of two slats of wood hinged together; the slats make a very loud smacking noise when slapped together. In *Commedia dell'arte* performances, the slapstick was used as a weapon which could provide a comically loud noise when hitting an actor with very little force.

A **crash box** is traditionally a covered wicker basket filled with pieces of broken glass. When dropped, it can

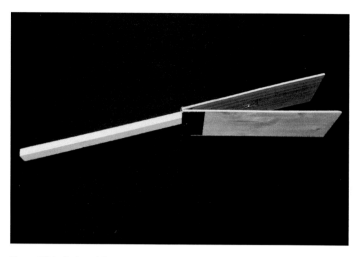

Figure 10-1: A slapstick.

sound like crashing or smashing. Broken china or seashells are safer substitutes for the glass. Other types of containers create different types of sound: a cardboard box will create a more muffled sound, while a metal trashcan filled with silverware will create a sharper rattling noise.

A **thunder sheet** (or thunder-plate) is a large sheet of thin steel hung from above. It is shaken from the bottom to create a resonant rumbling roar. Some of these can be over 12 feet tall. An oversized bass drum can be used for rolling thunder. Older theatres used a "thundercarriage," which is a cart filled with stones rolled around backstage.

A **rain box** is a long box filled with many ledges or rods in random locations. Before being closed, a number of dried peas or small pebbles are placed within. As the box is tilted, the peas rush over all the ledges, creating a natural smattering of sound. Smaller boxes can be held, while larger ones are attached on a center pivot and operated like a seesaw. A rain barrel operates

Figure 10-2: A thunder sheet.

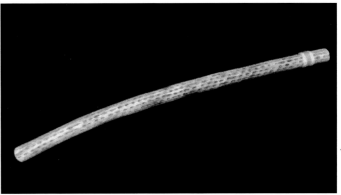

Figure 10-4: A rain stick operates on the same principle as a rain box.

Figure 10-3: A rain box, shown with one side removed. The peas are enlarged for clarity: a real rain box will have far more.

Figure 10-5: A wind machine.

Figure 10-6: A wooden ratchet noisemaker.

Sometimes a director wants to have a real gunshot sound come from offstage. As mentioned in Chapter 9, the use of firearms and blank ammunition on stage comes with a whole slew of safety and legal issues that this book does not cover. An offstage gunshot has the same potential for danger as an onstage gunshot.

with a similar concept, but in a wide cylinder which is continuously turned.

A **wind machine** is a hand-cranked barrel made of wooden slats. A piece of canvas or moire silk fabric is stretched over it. As the barrel is turned, it creates a whooshing noise. The sound can be modified by using different fabrics and by adjusting the tightness.

A **ratchet noisemaker** creates a loud clacking sound. A thin wooden slat snaps against cogs on a wheel as it is turned. For a more cacophonous noise, several can be attached to a single noisemaker.

Two wood blocks and a skilled operator can simulate the sound of horse hooves. Elastic bands can be used to attach the blocks to the operator's hands. Coconut halves are sometimes used, but the ends need to be cut perfectly flat and smooth. Two blocks covered in sandpaper can be rubbed together for train noises.

Many other ready-made devices are used to create sound in the theatre: bird whistles, duck calls, chimes, pipes, and bells. A few hours of experimentation with various objects and materials can reveal more sources for interesting sound effects.

Musical Instruments

Are musical instruments the responsibility of props? Many prop masters will argue they are not, but production managers still hand them off to us.

Whether musical instruments are provided by props varies widely from theatre to theatre, and many theatres will handle the matter on a case-by-case basis. If the instrument appears without being played, it is often provided by props. Many props departments will have a stock of common instruments they can pull from. If it actually needs to be played, it may be provided by the sound department or production management. Often, instruments become both the sound and props departments' responsibility. Sound will provide the instrument and necessary accessories, while props will alter the look (under sound's guidance) without affecting the acoustical qualities of the instrument.

If the actor is also a musician, their personal instrument might be rented for the show, and any consumables like reeds, strings, or picks are paid for by the theatre.

Musicians speak a whole other language from props, so if you find you are in charge of providing equipment for musicians, be sure to get them to specify the exact brand and type of accessories they need, whether drumsticks, reeds, mutes, or even guitar picks. They may all look the same to you, but they act differently for the musicians.

Maintenance is another issue that comes up with instruments in a show. This is usually beyond the skill set of a props department, and you should make sure someone else is handling the regular tuning and upkeep of the show's instruments.

Instruments' rentals, repair, and maintenance can take out a significant chunk of your budget, so always be sure you are not just getting all the responsibility dumped on you. Many prop directors will insist that anything beyond the appearance of an instrument on stage is not their responsibility.

The cost difference is immense too. Old trumpets can be found for less than $50, and upright pianos are often given away. It is no problem for a props department to clean them up and make them look new. But actual, concert-playable versions of these instruments cost thousands of dollars.

If the actor is not capable of playing the instrument, props may supply a dummy instrument, while the sound comes from a speaker or musician hidden nearby. The play may also need a historical or fantasy instrument which needs to be built from scratch. You may be able to hide an electric keyboard in a prop harpsichord, or build a fake carrot around a cheap whistle.

Speakers

If you want sound to come out of your prop that is cued by the sound board, you will need to get a speaker in there. Sound can be localized by the audience, so playing it through the general speakers in the house will not be as realistic or effective as the sound coming directly from the prop.

If the prop remains stationary and you can have a cord running to it, then it is quite simple for your sound department to run a speaker cable from offstage and plug it into a speaker inside the prop. If the prop is too small for a speaker, you can hide the speaker on a nearby piece of furniture, behind some set dressing, or within a piece of scenery.

Figure 10-7: This speaker is hidden behind a photo next to some books, with a doily over the top. It provided the source sound for the nonworking radio directly above it. *Having Our Say*, Triad Stage, 2017. Set design by Natalie Taylor Hart.

If the prop needs to move around stage, you may still use stationary speakers if the sound only happens during specific moments. Find out where the prop is located when it needs to create sound and hide a speaker nearby. If it makes sound in two locations, hide two speakers. If the prop generates sound while it moves around stage, or if the set design disallows hiding any speakers, then you may need to consider wireless speakers, which we will talk about soon.

The speaker should not be completely encased in solid material. The grill should remain as open as possible while still hiding it. Try to hide it where you can have an opening covered in fabric, a grill, or slats. If the fabric is pulled tight, it is possible to make it appear as a solid surface.

Practical Speakers

If sound needs to come from a prop such as a television or radio, it may be most realistic to use the prop's original speakers. Old TVs and radios have a particularly "tinny" quality to their sound that most audiences can recognize. Older models are especially easy to open up and find the wires that connect to the speaker. Hand it off to your sound department to connect to the theatre's system. They may need to reinforce the sound with additional nearby speakers.

Passive versus Active Speakers

A speaker needs three things to work: the speaker itself, an amplifier, and a power source. You will find two types of speakers: passive and active (sometimes called unpowered and powered, respectively).

This is more for the sound department than props; the sound emanating from the prop only has to be loud enough for the audience to localize the source. You can add volume and clarity by "feathering in" the same sound over the main theatre speakers. Playing the sound over the house speakers is useful as a backup too, in case the prop's speaker fails during a performance.

A **passive speaker** is driven by a separate amplifier located elsewhere. The amplifier requires a power source, but the speaker itself does not. Passive speakers are lighter and less expensive than comparable active speakers. They require only the cable coming from the amplifier to produce sound. Passive speakers are typically part of the theatre's permanent sound system and are handled by the sound department. These may be used when you can have a cord running to your prop.

An **active speaker** has the amplifier (and other circuitry) built in. They are more portable and easier to set up. They need both a cable coming from the sound source and a power cord (if AC-powered). A battery-powered active speaker is the most portable, and is what props people use for portable sound.

It is possible to power an AC-powered active speaker with an inverter and external battery, but the wrong kind of inverter or battery can lead to a hum over the speakers. Plus, that extra equipment makes it less portable. It will make your life so much easier to find a battery-powered speaker for your portable props.

Battery-Powered Speakers

Small battery-powered speakers for MP3 players and smartphones are perfect for props. Most come with a 3.5mm cord for hooking directly into an auxiliary audio output jack or headphone port of a music player or laptop. They can be as small as 3 inches (76mm) in diameter and 1¼ inches (31.75mm) tall. Some have built-in rechargeable batteries while others take regular AA or AAA cells. Even highly rated brands like iTour and iHome can be found for under $20. Be aware that some of these speakers have a "sleep mode" to save battery life after a few minutes of inactivity. They can take one or two seconds to wake back up again, which is not useful for precise sound cues.

If you need more sound and can deal with a larger size, you can start looking at personal monitors, battery-powered guitar amps, and other speakers made for portable location audio, referencing, or small venues. Again, you want a battery-powered, active speaker for standalone portability. Many of these will have input jacks for ¼″ audio or XLR cables. If your playback device has a 3.5mm port, you will need either a 3.5mm-to-¼″ adapter or a cable with 3.5mm on one end and ¼″ on the other.

Getting the Sound to the Speakers

The sound for your speakers needs to come from somewhere. You can have a small playback device hidden on the prop itself and controlled from there, or the sound can be cued and played from the theatre's sound board.

Small playback devices have become devilishly simple in a short amount of time. You can now find a device that plays MP3, WAV, and WMA audio, fits in the palm of your hand, and costs less than $10.

Of course, you do not just want to get the cheapest one you can find. You want something that can be controlled easily by the actor or crew member. Find one with larger buttons that are easy to find and that cannot accidentally be pressed beforehand. Some media players come with a small remote control that can be attached to the outside of the prop or used by a crew member offstage.

You want to be able to start and stop the sound on cue. Some of the cheaper models will endlessly loop through the files rather than stopping automatically when the file is finished playing. You want one that gives you the control you need.

A media player will either have a slot for a memory card, a USB connector to download files directly from a computer, or both.

You also want a player with enough battery life to last through a performance. Some will go into a "sleep mode" after a few minutes of inactivity, and take a few seconds to wake back up when you need to play the cue.

A button-activated sound recorder is another cheap and easy way to get a sound effect into a prop. They are self-contained devices usually used for putting sounds in plush toys, scrapbooks, and other hobbies. You have to use the built-in recorder: you cannot just load up prerecorded sounds. The speakers are not always great, though you can open them up and run the wires to a different speaker.

Figures 10-8 and 10-9: An audio trigger board allows you to wire on buttons or sensors to play prerecorded sounds. The board may either have a memory card slot for external memory or a USB port to upload sounds to internal memory. Assigning the sounds to the various pins is typically accomplished by giving the files specific names (for instance, on this board, naming a sound file "T03.wav" will make it play when pin 3 is triggered). More expensive boards even have DMX compatibility.

Figure 10-10: A small wireless speaker connected to the headphone jack of a wireless in-ear monitor receiver is small enough to fit inside a baby doll to make it cry on cue. The iTour speaker in this photo is only 3 inches (76mm) in diameter. The transmitter is connected to the sound board by your sound department.

Most often though, a sound designer wants to cue the sound from the sound board, so you will need to hook the speaker into the theatre's system. You can plug it in with a cord, which kind of defeats the purpose of having a wireless speaker to begin with. For true portability, you will also need a wireless transmitter and receiver to send the audio signal to your speaker.

A wireless in-ear monitoring system (IEM) has small receivers that can hook up to a small speaker. They cost several hundred dollars, but your theatre may already have them, or they can be rented. They have a 3.5mm jack for connecting to headphones, but you can connect directly to a battery-powered speaker.

Other wireless speaker systems exist; many are used for home theatre systems. With many of these, the wireless receiver is built into the speaker, so you cannot choose a different size or shape of speaker. You also need to test the wireless reliability and range in your theatre space.

Bluetooth Speakers

A lot of tiny wireless speakers you find today use Bluetooth. A Bluetooth speaker eliminates the need for a separate wireless receiver, making it one of the tiniest ways to get sound into a prop. You do need a Bluetooth transmitter on your soundboard. You can also have a Bluetooth media player or smartphone backstage if you do not need to cue the effect from the soundboard.

Bluetooth speakers have several disadvantages that make them one of the least ideal solutions for wireless sound. The range is not too great: the typical range is about 30 feet (9m), but physical obstacles and interference from other wireless devices can cut that down. Some theatres find Bluetooth is unreliable past six feet (1.8m).

Bluetooth can also disconnect randomly. A frequent cause of this is other Bluetooth devices in the vicinity searching for connections. Your audience may have a plethora of Bluetooth devices in their pockets, all searching for new connections. Good luck convincing everyone to turn them all off!

Finally, Bluetooth speakers have a lag between the sound cue being played and the sound coming out of the speaker. Precise cuing with Bluetooth is nearly impossible.

Their advantage is the cheap price, ready availability, and tiny form factor. If you have a small venue and do not need precisely cued sound, you can run to any store with electronic accessories and pick up a Bluetooth speaker. Most theatres and sound departments will ask you to avoid them though.

Phone Ringing

Analog phones have a built-in bell that will ring when supplied with the correct electrical signal.

The Tele-Q is the go-to device for making a phone ring on stage. You simply run a telephone cord from your phone to the Tele-Q, which is powered either by AC or batteries. It has a single button on the outside; pushing it makes the phone ring. If the telephone being used is fully operational, it will stop ringing as soon as the handset is picked up.

With a Tele-Q, the operator controls the pattern of the ring, so they will need to be taught which pattern to use; a US phone and a UK phone ring with different patterns.

You can also find tutorials online on building your own phone ringer. Wireless dimmers like the RC4 also allow you to ring a phone directly from the light board.

Figure 10-11: A Tele-Q connected to a rotary phone.

Ringing Cell Phone

A ringing cell phone is the bane of many a prop person's existence. Most phones need to both light up and produce sound. Directors often want the phone to start ringing automatically, but stop ringing by the actor triggering it. You can find many potential solutions out there, but not many integrate well into how a theatre works.

The easiest options involve buying or downloading an app to control a real working smartphone. Many apps which allow you to fake a call on a cell phone require the actor to trigger their own phone. This is often too demanding, and does not allow you to ring a phone which is in their pocket or sitting on a piece of furniture.

The most reliable app used by many theatres today is called StageCaller. It allows you to trigger any iOS (like the iPhone) or Android phone over WIFI. You will want a dedicated WIFI router separate from what theatre staff and patrons use to access the internet. It takes a bit of testing and configuring to get all the settings on the sound board, network, and cell phone absolutely correct, but the results can be very reliable and consistent.

You can try to just call the cell phone from another cell phone. However, even in the best of situations, there is quite a significant lag between the time one phone dials and the other begins to ring. Many theatres also suffer from spotty cell reception. Finally, having an active cell phone on stage leaves the risk of it ringing from an outside call or buzzing because of a text message or other notification. This method has so many drawbacks that it is rarely useful other than as a last-minute addition to a one-off performance at a fringe festival.

You can hide a speaker on the actor's costume and have the ringtone come from there. A small speaker hidden on set can also be used if the actor does not move around a lot. Realistically, an audience cannot pinpoint the precise location of a ringing cell phone, so the speaker can be a few feet away and the audience will not notice. However, this method will not make a phone light up or vibrate.

If you really need the phone to light up but cannot make an app work, you can try using a dummy phone with LEDs inside the screen that are cued wirelessly in conjunction with the localized speaker. Dummy or display phones are fairly cheap if you search online, though you may also find them for free from a cell-phone store when they are discarding their older models.

You may not even need a dummy phone: a cheap phone case wrapped around a rectangle of Plexiglas looks just like a phone from the audience.

eleven

control (remote, micro, practical)

The prop effects we have discussed throughout this book can all be triggered manually, either by an actor or a crew member nearby. Switches and buttons can start electrical components, and manual effects can be started by pulling a string, flipping a lever, or pushing a rod. However, you may need more sophisticated ways to control your effect. It may need to be wireless because no one is around to trigger it. It may need to be cued by the light board for timing with other elements. It may need a microcontroller to allow complex controlling of multiple components.

This chapter will start with DMX, which is the communication used by theatrical light boards. Next, we will look at wireless DMX controllers. We will discuss radio control and other wireless control methods which are independent of the light board. Finally, we will take a look at microcontrollers, such as the Arduino.

Who Controls the Prop?

If a prop lights up, it should be controlled by the light board. If a prop makes sound, it should be controlled by the sound board.

Other types of effects, even if it is possible to control them from the light board, should be on their own control. We like to keep the control of effects in their own little "worlds." In some cases, you can have the stage manager or crew trigger the effect. Build a little control box, which could be as simple as mounting a remote control to a piece of wood with a label.

The electricians and lighting designer need to check through all the lights and run through cues, sometimes rapidly and repeatedly. A prop effect cued by the light board would be triggered multiple times as they did

this. Imagine if a complicated breakaway effect takes 20 minutes to set up and uses expensive consumables, and five minutes before curtain, the light board operator inadvertently flips to that cue and sets it off!

DMX

DMX-512 (which I'll just call DMX) is the international standard for digital communication of theatrical lights and effects. DMX is how the light board tells the lights when to turn on and how bright to be. It can also communicate with more complicated devices, such as color-changing LEDs and moving lights.

Many performance venues have **preinstalled circuitry** used to connect theatrical lighting to the dimmers. When a prop needs to plug in, an electrician will run a cable from this preinstalled circuitry to your prop. The **dimmers** are controlled by the lighting board through DMX. It controls the output of the light with a number between 0 and 255. "Off" is zero, 50 percent brightness is 128, and fully on (or just "full") is 255.

Incandescent and halogen bulbs can be dimmed. Other types of electronics may be damaged if you dim them, especially DC props with an AC-adaptor and many motors. In these cases, make sure your electrician attaches them to a **non-dim** (if available). A non-dim is connected to the light board just like a dimmer, but only allows a device to be on or off.

You can find many devices which are controlled directly by DMX, like foggers, servos, and pneumatic valves. You can also buy hardware which adds DMX control to other devices, such as turning a regular LED strip into one that can be controlled by your light board. DMX can control parameters other than brightness; for

Figure 11-1: A plug box is a common type of power distribution found in many theatres. The outlets are labeled so the electrician knows which dimmer will control the device. Plug boxes and other types of preinstalled circuitry are in fixed locations, so the locations of any props being plugged in should be made known to the electrician as soon as possible. If you wait until after they plug in all their lights, there might not be any plug boxes near your prop, and they will need to waste time running a very long cable from another part of the theatre (if they have one).

instance, it can change the color on a multi-color LED strip. DMX-enabled devices need one cable for the power and a second cable for the DMX signal.

The downside of DMX is that it does not have any ability to check and correct errors. Bad wiring or excessive static electricity can trigger a device accidentally. For a light, this is annoying, but not dangerous; for a moving prop or an air cannon, it can be hazardous if it accidentally goes off when an actor is in the wrong place and not expecting it. The DMX standard prohibits the use of DMX where the absence of error checking can lead to a hazard in human health.

Another downside of building a DMX-controlled prop is that you need to be in your theatre to run it from the light board. You can buy small DMX controllers to test your prop in your shop, though they are somewhat pricey.

You can even send and receive DMX from an Arduino (or other microcontroller) for super fancy effects. Of course, if you can do that, you probably do not need to read this chapter. The Arduino can be used to translate the DMX into commands for your components, or it can be a simple trigger for a series of effects which are too complex and fast for the light board to enact. DMX only updates commands 44 times a second.

For props controlled by DMX, most of the programming and setup is done by the lighting department. The information is presented here to help you communicate with your electrician and to help you anticipate problems while in the planning phase. If you ever need to design a prop effect which you think should be triggered and run from the light board, start the communication with your electrician as early as possible.

Wireless Dimmers

A wireless dimmer has a DMX signal transmitted from a transceiver to a small dimmer unit. The transceiver is connected to your light board and the dimmer goes into your prop. Some wireless dimmers are small enough to fit inside an electric candlestick, allowing you to turn it on and off, fade its brightness, and even run a preprogrammed flicker sequence.

Two popular brands of wireless dimmer products are RC4 and City Theatrical. Each has a wide range of wireless devices for various purposes.

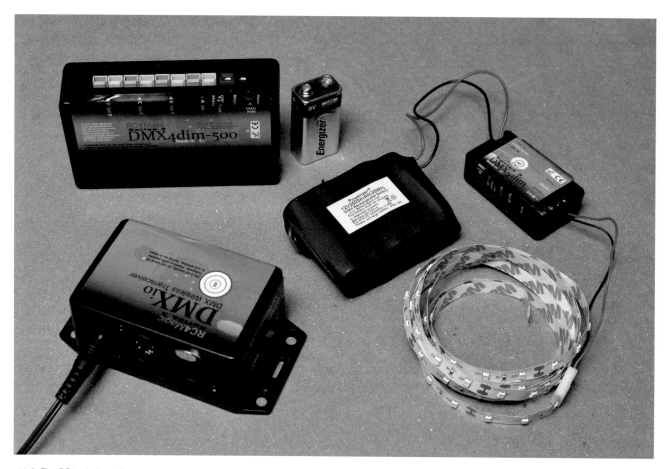

Figure 11-2: The RC4 wireless dimmer comes in a four-channel version (top) and a two-channel version (right). The transmitter (bottom left) connects to the lightboard with a DMX cable. On the two-channel receiver, you can see how the battery connects to the DC inputs on one side, and the device being controlled is connected on the other.

The wireless dimmer connects to a battery for a power source. It is made to accept a range of voltages (6 to 35VDC for RC4, 7.5 to 30VDC for City Theatrical). If you want to control a 12V LED strip, hook the dimmer to a 12V battery and connect the LED strip to the dimmer.

Most wireless dimmers come with either two channels or four channels. A four-channel dimmer can control either four individual components, or four different parts of a single device; for instance, with an RGBW LED strip, a four-channel dimmer can control the red, green, blue, and white LEDs separately.

In most wireless dimmers, you connect bare wire leads from your components. Some high-powered wireless dimmers come with built-in connectors instead.

Figures 11-3 and 11-4: This LED cube is controlled by an RC4 wireless dimmer, allowing it to change brightness and color while an actor carries it around. *The World According to Snoopy.* Photos courtesy of Erin Kehr.

Radio Control

Radio control uses frequencies within the electromagnetic spectrum to communicate wirelessly. It requires a transmitter to send the signal and a receiver to pick it up. In the simplest systems, an **RF** (radio frequency) transmitter consists of a single button, which sends a command to an RF receiver which acts as an on-off switch. More complicated systems like an **RC** (radio controlled) airplane can have a transmitter filled with multiple joysticks and buttons that precisely control several servos and motors on the receiver.

An RF transmitter will encode its signals so that it is only paired with a specific receiver. Most receivers allow you to "teach" them the encoding, so you can pair several transmitters with a single receiver (in case one gets lost), or pair several receivers with one transmitter (to allow simultaneous control of multiple props from one button).

The use of radio frequencies is regulated by whatever country you are transmitting from. Most low-power hobbyist RF transmitters we use in props operate in frequencies which are either unregulated or do not require a license. Always double-check the legality of your devices though, particularly if you are building props that will tour to other countries.

Your theatre is filled with many other wireless devices all competing for frequency: wireless headsets, wi-fi, Bluetooth speakers, and more. When your audience arrives, it is a veritable soup of interference between all their cell phones and other devices. Some devices cannot broadcast through all that interference. A radio control unit may work well in one theatre space but not in another, even if the distance between transmitter and receiver remains the same. Always test your radio-controlled props in as close to show conditions as possible, and be ready with a backup plan should they fail.

An **ASK Radio** (Amplitude-shift keying) is a very cheap one-way radio which transmits between 300 and 440MHz. These can be a bit unreliable for crucial effects or in large performance venues, but for simple effects in mid-sized theatres, they save a lot of time and money.

Zigbee is a communications protocol for radio-based networks, and the most common Zigbee devices are **Xbee radio modules**. Unlike the one-way ASK radio, Xbee modules can communicate in both directions; you can even have more than two all talking back and forth with each other. They transmit serial data, meaning they can send complex instructions rather than just a simple on or off command.

Configuring and controlling Xbee radio modules is far too complex to get into here. I do not know of any props people who use them regularly, but holiday display and theme park people use them a lot. You can find many tutorials and forums online for using the software and hooking them up to various microcontrollers.

Infrared

Infrared (IR) remotes are the kind used for televisions and other home electronics. Their main disadvantage is that they need a clear line of sight between the remote and the receiver, and they do not work over too great a distance.

Their advantage is that other radio frequencies will not interfere with them. The only thing that can cause interference are electronic ballast fluorescent lights.

Figure 11-5: The HD2RX is a cheap and reliable ASK Radio that controls two channels. The transmitter is a small two-button fob similar to a keyless entry remote on an automobile. Here, the board triggers a solenoid, which opens the jaws of these locking pliers.

Figure 11-6: A battery-powered candle with an infrared remote.

Microcontrollers

A **microcontroller** (MCU) is a tiny computer that you can stick inside your prop. It can be used to control anything electrical, such as lights, motors, valves, and sound.

They hold a program which you write on your regular computer. You write the program, compile it, then upload it to the microcontroller.

You can find tons of different microcontrollers out there, with names like Basic Stamp, AVR, HC11, and PIC. Some can only be programmed once, which is not very useful to us. Some need a special ultraviolet eraser to reprogram them. Others can be reprogrammed again and again just by overwriting the code. Some require additional hardware to enable you to transfer the program from your computer to the microcontroller.

One of the more popular hobbyist microcontrollers in recent years is the Arduino. It is endlessly reprogrammable, and you can upload the program straight from your computer using a USB cable. It is faster and far cheaper than its predecessors.

Suppose you want an LED to blink. You can have a button controlled by a crew member who manually turns it on and off to blink it. If you want it to blink on its own without a microcontroller, you would need to construct a circuit using capacitors, transistors, or maybe a 555 timer IC. To change the rate at which the LED blinked, you would have to physically alter the circuit, and perhaps purchase completely different components.

A microcontroller sits between the power supply and your LED and takes the place of all those components. If you want the LED to blink at a different rate, you alter the program and reupload it to the microcontroller. You can have a row of LEDs that follow a chase sequence, with a puff of smoke at the end. If you wanted to change the order in which they light up or when the puff of smoke occurs, just rewrite the program; none of the components need to be rewired or replaced.

For more complexity, you can attach sensors to the microcontroller so that the components can react to stimuli such as sound, light, buttons, etc.

Props people use microcontrollers like the Arduino to give their props complicated light and motion sequences. For instance, you can fill mason jars with many individual LEDs and use the Arduino to light them up in a manner that simulates fireflies. A microcontroller can be used to speed up or slow down a clock motor to control the time on a clock, or a disco ball motor to make the disco ball spin in sync with lights and music. A very complex example where a microcontroller is useful is a fake "bomb" which has an LED countdown clock. The microcontroller controls the clock itself, and when it reaches zero, the bomb lights up and a small fog effect is triggered.

Figure 11-7: The Arduino Duemilanove has 14 Digital IO (input/output) pins along the top (where the LED is connected). Six of those are also Analog Out pins. Along the bottom are six Analog In pins. It has a USB port to connect to your computer or for providing power. It also has a 2.1mm barrel port for connecting an AC adapter or 9V battery.

A microcontroller is limited in the number of outputs it has as well as the amount of current it can supply. You can put multiple components on a single output, but you still cannot exceed the maximum current without damaging the board. For example, the Arduino operates at 5V and can only run a maximum current of 200mA at a single time. Low voltage components like LEDs, small servos, computer fans, and EL wire are alright to run directly from a microcontroller. If you need to control heavy-duty components like incandescent lights, pneumatic solenoids, or larger motors, you will need to pair a relay with the microcontroller. Relays are explained later in this chapter.

Programming a Microcontroller

Writing code can be tricky if you have never done it before. It requires a different way of thinking. A computer requires everything to be defined and every step to be completely explicit. Imagine you need a 1x4 to be

16 inches long. You tell your best carpenter, "cut this board to 16 inches," and she can do it. Writing code is more like telling the world's worst intern to cut the board. The instructions might be more like:

```
 1 Put on your dust mask
 2 Put on your safety glasses
 3 Take a pencil and ruler
 4 Measure 16 inches from one end of the board
 5 Make a mark
 6 Carry the board to the chop saw
 7 Place the board firmly against the fence
 8 Line the side of the blade up to the waste side
   of the mark
 9 Place your left hand on the board
10 Place your right hand on the saw
11 Hold the button to turn the saw on
12 Lower the saw into the wood
13 Release the button when the saw has cut through
   the wood
14 Let the saw back up
```

These instructions may need further clarification depending on how bad your intern is. Questions like "How should I carry the board?" or "What button do I push?" may require you to rewrite or add steps to the instructions.

Writing code is like this. Further, the syntax needs to be exact and correct. Missing even a single semicolon can prevent the code from functioning.

Arduino code is easy to learn if you are familiar with object-oriented programming languages. Basic Stamp, another popular type of microcontroller, is easy to learn if you are familiar with the BASIC language.

Let us look at some example code to make an LED blink.

	Basic Stamp	Arduino
1	' Making an LED blink	// Making an LED blink
2		
3	' {$STAMP BS2}	void setup()
4	' {$PBASIC 2.5}	{
5		pinMode(13, OUTPUT);
6	Main:	}
7	HIGH 15	
8	PAUSE 1000	void loop()
9	LOW 15	{
10	PAUSE 1000	digitalWrite(13, HIGH);
11	GOTO Main	delay(1000);
12		digitalWrite(13, LOW);
13		delay(1000);
14		}

Both of these codes end up with the same result from the viewer's end, but go about them differently. Let's look at Basic Stamp first.

The first line is a comment. A **comment** is like an aside directed to the audience but not heard by other characters. It is meant to be read by a human looking at the program and ignored by the computer. In Basic Stamp, anything to the right of an apostrophe creates a comment. Adding comments is helpful if someone else needs to look at your code, or even just to remind yourself why you did something when you edit the code later.

Lines 3 and 4, while also comments, are necessary for every Basic Stamp program. They are directives which tell the BASIC Stamp Editor which microcontroller you are using and what version of the programming language you are working in.

We now begin the actual program. Line 6 simply labels the line as "Main," which will come in handy in a second. The next line tells the microcontroller to turn pin

15 to "high." If your LED's anode (the positive, longer leg) is connected to pin 15 on the microcontroller, this command turns it on. "High" just means it sends all the voltage available to it, which in the case of the Basic Stamp is 5V. The other option is "Low," which in this case is 0V. It is easier to think of it in terms of "on" and "off," but you have to write "high" and "low."

Line 8 pauses the program for 1,000 milliseconds, or one second. The LED remains on. Line 9 switches pin 15 to "low," turning the LED off. Then, we pause again for another second.

Line 11 tells the program to go to the line labelled "Main." The program repeats. The program will loop through this code until you disconnect the power.

Now let us look at the Arduino code. Line 1 is a comment. Anything after a double forward slash "//" is a comment. The rest of the code consists of two functions.

A **function** is a set of instructions. In Arduino code, like in many object-oriented programming languages, a function is encapsulated within a set of curly brackets. Lines 3 to 6 define the function called "setup."

Going back to our set of instructions for the world's worst intern, we can make that a function called "cutToLength." We can define it by typing

```
void cutToLength()
 {
 (all the instructions in our previous
example...)
 }
```

Then, if we ever need the intern to cut another piece, we can just write

```
cutToLength();
```

and it will refer to the function for the list of instructions.

Arduino code requires at least two functions in every code you upload to the microcontroller: setup() and loop(). The setup function executes once when the Arduino is turned on, and then the loop function executes over and over again until the power is turned off.

In our example, the setup function sets pin 13 to an output; these pins can also be inputs (used for sensors and buttons), but we just want to send current out to the LED. Your LED needs to have its anode connected to pin 13 for this to work. The digitalWrite() command allows you to change pin 13 to "high." In Line 11, we give it a delay of 1000, which, like the BASIC Stamp, is in milliseconds. Line 12 sets pin 13 back to "low," followed by another one second delay. You do not need a "goto" command, as everything within the curly brackets of the loop() function will automatically repeat.

You will note that every command in Arduino code other than comments (and a few specialized ones) ends in a semicolon. The spacing and line breaks within the function are merely to make the code easier to read and follow. You can write lines 3 through 6 as

```
void setup(){ pinMode(13, OUTPUT); }
```

and the code would do the same thing.

Here we use a breadboard to hook up three LEDs to the Arduino. The anodes of each LED are connected to a different digital IO pin, while all the cathodes lead back to the GND (ground) pin. We change the setup() function to define all the pins, than write a simple little chase sequence in the loop() function.

Figure 11-8: This Arduino is connected to a breadboard and a battery pack.

```
// A 3 LED chase sequence
void setup()
{
 pinMode(11, OUTPUT);
 pinMode(12, OUTPUT);
 pinMode(13, OUTPUT);
}
void loop()
{
 digitalWrite(11, HIGH);
 delay(1000);
 digitalWrite(11, LOW);
 digitalWrite(12, HIGH);
 delay(1000);
 digitalWrite(12, LOW);
 digitalWrite(13, HIGH);
 delay(1000);
 digitalWrite(13, LOW);
 digitalWrite(12, HIGH);
 delay(1000);
 digitalWrite(12, LOW);
}
```

If we wanted to speed it up, we just go in and decrease the delay.

This has been the most rudimentary introduction to programming possible. The great thing about code is that you can find many examples and snippets online from people who have already solved many of the same problems you will face. You can simply copy and paste what you need, adapt it, and upload it to your microcontroller.

You can find libraries to help you out. A **library** is a collection of routines which your program can use without having to program them all from scratch. For example, the Arduino *servo* library gives you a number of functions for controlling servo motors with the Arduino.

```
#include <Servo.h> // adds the servo library
Servo myservo;
void setup()
{
 myservo.attach(9); // sets pin 9 to control a
servo
 myservo.write(90); // set servo position to mid-
point
}
void loop() {}
```

The Arduino software comes included with a number of libraries you can import directly from the menu. You can also search online for libraries to download, or create your own.

Recordable Prop Controllers

A recordable prop controller is a simpler (though more expensive) way to control electronics without having to program anything. You connect your lights, motors, valves, and other components to the board. You hit record on the controller and "perform" the effect in real time, using buttons to turn your components on and off. Once recorded, the controller will play back the effect whenever it is triggered, which can be done by a button or sensor.

Think of it like recording a song on a keyboard, only instead of different notes, you are "playing" the lights, smoke puffs, and servos.

These are popular in the haunted house community, and boards come with names such as the PicoBoo and BooBox. Simple ones can record a two-minute loop controlling two different components, while more complicated boards can control up to 16 components for hours.

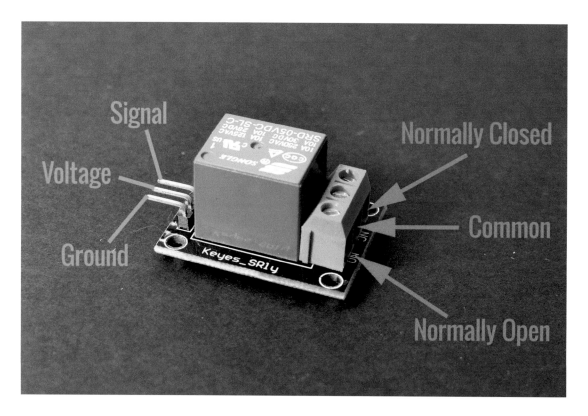

Figure 11-9: A relay on a breakout board. On the left are the pins to operate the relay; this particular model requires 5VDC to activate. On the right are connectors for the component being switched on. This model can handle up to 250VAC or 110VDC.

Relays

Microcontrollers and cheap RC boards can only send low-voltage DC signals, but you may want to control items like larger motors, AC lighting, or a magical vacuum cleaner. A **relay** is a switch which is triggered by a low-voltage DC signal, but turns a higher voltage AC or DC component on and off.

With a relay, you will need two power sources; the low-voltage DC power which is also controlling your microcontroller or RC board, and the higher voltage power source controlling the component itself. The two power supplies never touch each other; your microcontroller or RC board stays in its own world of low-voltage DC power, and will not be fried by the higher voltage power connected to your components.

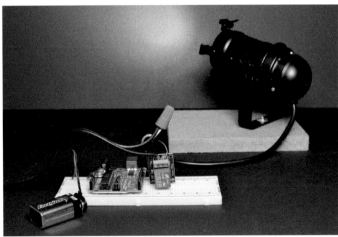

Figures 11-10 and 11-11: The relay is plugged into this breadboard so it uses the same power as the Arduino, and pin 13 on the Arduino is connected to the signal pin of the relay. The cord from the birdie is connected to the other side of the relay just like a regular SPST switch and plugged into the mains. We are using the exact same code found earlier in the chapter where pin 13 is switched from high to low every second. In this case, pin 13 is connected to the relay, so the birdie is flashing on and off once per second.

special note

Throughout the text, I make reference to brand names and specific companies that manufacture certain products. This is done to clarify; in many cases, the brand names are used generically, while in others, a brand name may be the only type of its product on the market. I do not mean to endorse these products or imply that they are superior to other products. Likewise, many of the photographs throughout the book show artisans brandishing brand-name tools and using brand-name machines. For the most part, the photograph was taken to illustrate a technique or a method, and the brand of the tool being used is what was available in the shop at the time. This book in no way claims any connection to or relationship with the manufacturers or distributors of any tools or products shown and discussed in this book.

Bibliography

The following is a list of books which I have found useful in researching this book. Some of the books are listed under the chapter of my book they best correspond to, though in some cases the information they contain may bridge several chapters.

Chapter 1: Designing, Prototyping, Testing

In many ways, the process for prototyping a trick prop is the same as the engineering design process. I gathered much of that information here:

"The Engineering Design Process." *Science Buddies*. Science Buddies, 11 Apr. 2011. Web. 26 June 2016. www.sciencebuddies.org/engineering-design-process/engineering-design-process-steps.shtml.

A good chunk of this chapter was first sketched out in a magazine article I wrote:

Hart, Eric. "Fast, Cheap, and Under Control." *Stage Directions*, June 2013: 14–15. Web. http://stage-directions.com/component/search/?searchword=eric%20hart&searchphrase=exact&Itemid=146.

Chapter 2: Electricity, Wiring, Soldering

McComb, Gordon. *Robot Builder's Bonanza*. 4th ed. New York: McGraw-Hill, 2011.

The SparkFun website (www.sparkfun.com) has a great many tutorials and guides to electrical components.

Chapter 3: Lights

Edman, Lenore. "Basics: Picking Resistors for LEDs." *Evil Mad Scientist Laboratories*. Evil Mad Scientist, 29 Aug. 2012. Web. 10 July 2016. www.evilmadscientist.com/2012/resistors-for-leds/.

Quindt, Svetlana. *The Book of Cosplay Lights: Getting Started with LEDs*. Germany: Self published, 2015.

Chapter 4: Motion

Roberts, Dustyn. *Making Things Move: DIY Mechanisms for Inventors, Hobbyists, and Artists*. New York: McGraw-Hill, 2010.

Chapter 5: Trick Mechanisms

Motley, Pseud. *Theatre Props*. New York: Drama Book Specialists, 1975.

- You can also find useful information on breakaways and lighting in this book.

Arnold, Richard L. *Scene Technology*. 3rd ed. Englewood Cliffs, NJ: Prentice-Hall, 1994.

Chapter 6: Pneumatics

Wise, Edwin. *Animatronics: A Guide to Animated Holiday Displays*. Indianapolis, IN: Prompt Publications, 2000.

- Also useful for motion and control.

Though mainly a store for parts, the website for Fright Props (www.frightprops.com) is filled with lot of great diagrams on assembling various pneumatic tricks.

Chapter 7: Liquid Delivery

James, Thurston. *The Theater Props Handbook: A Comprehensive Guide to Theater Properties, Materials, and Construction*. White Hall, VA: Betterway Publications, 1987.

Chapter 8: Breakaways

James, Thurston. *The Prop Builder's Molding & Casting Handbook*. Cincinnati, OH: Betterway, 1989.

Chapter 9: Smoke and Fire

Walne, Graham, ed. *Effects for the Theatre*. London: A & C Black, 1995.

- This book is also useful for motion, sound effects, and lighting effects.

The Actors' Equity Time and Distance Guidelines for Theatrical Smoke, Fog, and Haze is currently available at www.actorsequity.org/docs/safesan/TD_guidelines.pdf.

Chapter 11: Control (Remote, Micro, Practical)

Peoples, Ben. *Embedded Electronics for Theatre*. Pittsburgh, PA: Trinculo's Attic, 2012.

- This book has a good introduction to electricity as well.

Banzi, Massimo. *Getting Started with Arduino*. Sebastopol, CA: O'Reilly Media, 2008.

Overall

Carter, Paul Douglas. *Backstage Handbook: An Illustrated Almanac of Technical Information*. 3rd ed. Louisville, KY: Broadway, 1994.

- This book remains a valuable visual reference for the tools, hardware, and equipment we use in theatre.

Sammler, Bronislaw J., and Don Harvey, eds. *Technical Design Solutions for Theatre*. Woburn, MA: Focal Press, 2002.

- The three volumes of this series contain a variety of specific projects dealing with every topic in this book.

Davies, Gill. *Create Your Own Stage Effects*. New York: Back Stage, 1999.

The collective knowledge of the members of the Society of Properties Artisan Managers (S*P*A*M) was invaluable in putting this book together. (http://propmasters.org)

The Control Booth (www.controlbooth.com) forum also remains very useful for all manner of tricks and tips.

index

website

Your prop effects adventures continue at www.propeffectsguidebook.com! There you'll find:

- videos detailing tricks and techniques described in this book
- a link to the author's blog, Eric Hart's "Prop Agenda," where he documents his ongoing adventures in props
- information on his other book, *The Prop Building Guidebook: For Theatre, Film, and TV*

The book and website give you a complete cache of construction advice for all your prop needs. Have fun, be safe, and happy building!